NORTH CAR~
STATE BOARD OF COMM~
LIBRARI~
FORSYTH TECHNICAL CC

D1036205

**NEA
EARLY CHILDHOOD
EDUCATION SERIES**

Teacher-Parent Partnerships to Enhance School Success in Early Childhood Education

Kevin J. Swick

A Joint Publication of
National Education Association
Southern Association on Children Under Six
(Division for Development)

The Author

Kevin J. Swick is Professor of Education at the University of South Carolina, Columbia. He is the author of *Maintaining Productive Student Behavior, Parents and Teachers as Discipline Shapers, A Proactive Approach to Discipline, Stress and Teaching, Student Stress: A Classroom Management System,* and *Discipline: Toward Positive Student Behavior;* and the coauthor of *Teacher Renewal* and *Parenting,* published by NEA.

The Advisory Panel

Nancy E. Bacot, Instructor, Elementary-Early Childhood Education, Arkansas State University, State University, Arkansas

Richard L. Biren, Elementary School Counselor, Brush, Colorado

Milly Cowles, Distinguished Professor Emerita, Newman, Georgia

Arlene Lewis Dykes, Third Grade Teacher, Claremont, New Hampshire

Sharon Elton, Early Childhood Teacher, Wilson Elementary School, Spokane, Washington

Donna Foglia, Kindergarten Teacher, Evergreen School District, San Jose, California

John M. Johnston, Professor of Early Childhood Teacher Education, Memphis State University, Tennessee

Karen Robertson, Associate Professor of Early Childhood Education and Assistant Dean, University of South Carolina at Spartanburg

Barbara J. Schram, Early Childhood Educator, Grand Ledge, Michigan

Margaret G. Weiser, Professor and Fellow, Regents' Center for Early Developmental Education, University of Northern Iowa, Cedar Falls

**NEA
EARLY CHILDHOOD
EDUCATION SERIES**

Teacher-Parent Partnerships to Enhance School Success in Early Childhood Education

Kevin J. Swick

LIBRARY
FORSYTH TECHNICAL COMMUNITY COLLEGE
2100 SILAS CREEK PARKWAY
WINSTON-SALEM, NC 27103-5197

A Joint Publication of
National Education Association
Southern Association on Children Under Six
(Division for Development)

Copyright © 1991
National Education Association of the United States

Printing History
    First Printing: October 1991

Note

The opinions expressed in this publication should not be construed as representing the policy or position of the National Education Association. Materials published by the NEA Professional Library are intended to be discussion documents for educators who are concerned with specialized interests of the profession.

Library of Congress Cataloging-in-Publication Data

Swick, Kevin J.
    Teacher-parent partnerships to enhance school success in early childhood education / Kevin J. Swick.
        p. cm.—(NEA early childhood education series)
        Includes bibliographical references (p.) and index.
        ISBN 0-8106-0363-2
        1. Early childhood education—United States—Parent participation.
    2. Parent-teacher relationships—United States. I. Title.
    II. Series: Early childhood education series (Washington, D.C.)
    LB1139.35.P37S94 1991
    372.11'03—dc20   91–21425
                                                                    CIP

372.11
Suoi
1991

CONTENTS

15.75

Chapter 1

INTRODUCTION

The helping professions and society are broadening their understanding of the significance of the early childhood years. During the past fifty years our knowledge of how children develop and learn has increased dramatically, prompting fresh insights on how to increase the child's potential for growth and offering many opportunities for teachers (the term *teacher* as used throughout this book is inclusive of the roles of caregivers) and parents to make these years happy and meaningful for children.

This dimension of *opportunity*, as it is being developed in early intervention efforts, offers new hope relative to the empowerment of future generations. Some examples of the possibilities that exist when the early years are of high quality follow:

- Prenatal health care, when carried out in a preventive and consistent manner, has a positive influence on the long-term well-being of the child (106).*
- Healthy attachments to loving and competent adults during the infant and toddler years strengthen the child's mental and emotional fabric (47, 64).
- Appropriate and meaningful language, social, and cognitive experiences increase children's competence for relating effectively to their environment (45, 58).

Unfortunately, the early childhood period also has a *risk* dimension that is seen in the negative influence that many factors have on children. For example, the damaging impact on children of poverty and poor health care is visible in their development, often delaying or inhibiting their healthy functioning (58). Just

*Numbers in parentheses appearing in the text refer to the Bibliography beginning on page 167.

as damaging are the superficial attempts to create super children through highly institutionalized and rigid academic early learning programs. Such attempts create unrealistic and unreachable expectations for young children (7, 66). Another risk factor for many children during these formative years is the dramatic weakening of their family and community ecology (86). Alarming increases in poverty, child abuse, neglect, and illiteracy are eroding the integrity of the child's social and spiritual fabric (106).

The central figures in fostering the potential of the early years of life are the *significant adults* in the child's world (7). Young children's avenues toward healthy development are linked to the skills and commitments of these adults (9). In this regard, adults provide the critical elements that combine to create growth and learning opportunities: provisions for basic care (inclusive of health, safety, and sustenance); access to continuing loving and nurturing relationships; involvement in appropriate and meaningful learning experiences; and the availability of individuals who provide guidance related to children's interactions with other environments (66).

Usually parents (or a surrogate parent) are the most significant adults children have access to as they experience childhood. Parents provide (or fail to provide) the leadership so critical to the child's healthy development. Decisions related to every aspect of the child's early life (birthing, nutrition, care, health, emotional support, learning opportunities, and relationships with others) are strongly influenced by parent involvement (92). Parents provide children with an initial framework to use in negotiating developmental and ecological issues. The diverse frameworks that come from different parenting styles can be either enabling or disabling, depending on their substance. Consider the two developmental areas of psychosocial and physical growth. Caldwell (cited in Blazer [9]) describes the patterns of the early life experiences of Geraldine.

Geraldine, weighing twenty pounds at eighteen months, weighed only two pounds at birth. Her mother was not quite sixteen at the time. The baby was cared for by a maternal great-aunt for two months, at which time the mother took her back to live with her and the maternal grandmother. After three months, the mother (then back in school) decided to release the child for adoption but refused to allow the aunt to have the baby. No adoptive home could be found and no settlement was reached. Within the first year of life Geraldine was in at least six different child care arrangements. (pp. 61, 62)

Clearly, Geraldine's early childhood context is permeated by factors that put her at risk. Essential to the development of trust, which is absolutely critical to healthy emotional and spiritual development, is the continuity and nurturance inherent in consistent, loving, parent-infant relationships, obviously lacking in Geraldine's life. Further, it is known that risk in one area of development can create or contribute to risk in other areas. Inadequate psychosocial development is often related to corresponding delays in physical growth, such as low body weight, severe coordination problems, and poor general health (35).

In a different, yet not dissimilar, context, we meet Raphael. His mother Rene is not quite 18, living with Raphael at her parent's home—the same house in which she grew up. Her boyfriend left her six months before Raphael was born. Beyond the normal issues that emerge in "teen families" that reside within the family of origin, a stable and nurturing environment is present, a setting and climate conducive to both Raphael's and Renee's growth. At his 12–month checkup, Raphael received a positive evaluation in all areas, including responsiveness—a key indicator of one's developmental status. Mother was doing well too, working to complete a computer programming course and enjoying being a mother. She has maintained her peer friendships but altered the composite of her life toward acquiring a needed sense of adult competence.

Several insights germane to successful parenting and early childhood development are evident in the stories about Rene and Raphael. *Perhaps the most significant factor is the critical influence of positive emotional and social relationships as they emerge in the lives of children and parents* (119). An ecology of well-being is seemingly at work in Rene's life, albeit not in any superficial manner. Seemingly at ease with her own growth and with her temporary yet positive "family within a family" arrangement, she is making positive decisions as exemplified in her care of Raphael and in her pursuit of her own educational and continuing socioemotional development Parental self-image and parental participation in competence-inducing endeavors are signficantly related to children's healthy development (108).

While not as evident as many of the observable well-being issues of parent and child development, establishment of a workable change-continuity scheme is vital to successful ventures in families (101). Raphael's life appears to be evolving within a system where a healthy balance between change and continuity are being formed. Certainly he will experience the usual life transitions that are inherent in development; yet, unlike Geraldine, Raphael is experiencing the emotional and physical security of an arrangement in which love and nurturance are continuous and sustained events in his life. The uniquely spiritual/emotional processes of attachment and human bonding occur best when the relationships within the family are consistently harmonious and yet open to growth and problem solving (9, 37, 47).

A significant element of the change-continuity process in which children need varying yet supportive experiences is the growth that is inherent in increasingly complex relationships (66). It is impossible for children to carry out long-term successful engagements in their environment without the strong support and guidance of significant adults, especially their very first teachers—parents. Observations and analyses of children who have benefited from healthy family arrangements indicate that intensive parental nurturance and leadership provide the foundation by which children initiate and sustain their growth during the early years (110). Indeed, recent research suggests that the power of the family is truly lifelong (66, 101).

Just as children need an intimate partnership with their parents, so too do parents need a close physical and psychological network of supportive and guiding relationships (37, 92). Parents also must negotiate continuing growth experiences in order to have the sustenance of meaningful self and self-environments to share and use in their leadership roles. Both the physical and psychological energy that emanates from past and present intergenerational relationships is a powerful force in parental development. Fraiberg (35) and, more recently, Rossi and Rossi (101) offer substantial evidence of the pervasive influence of intergenerational family experiences on the way parents carry out their own parenting. For example, the commitment to roles such as nurturing, guiding, and teaching appear to be embedded in these intergenerational patterns of life (101). Clearly, parents and children are sustained in their developmental experiences through the many benefits that arise from strong, positive relationships with the generation network that embraces their lives (40).

What has been learned from the study of intergenerational influences on parents and children is also applicable to the family's relationships with other social systems: child care, school, church, neighborhood, friends, work, and the larger systems of the community (11, 27, 41). Parents and children need support structures that strengthen their family bonds as well as assist them in extending their development through meaningful involvement in other social contexts. These support structures play a crucial role in cultures that are highly complex. Research indicates, for example, that high-quality child care not only influences children's lives positively but also strengthens the fabric of the entire family (86). In a similar manner, productive family-school relationships appear to increase the involvement of children and parents in school and community activities (20). This process of acquiring and using skills and competencies in contexts beyond their immediate family is critically related to the many "partnerships" parents and children are able to construct during the early childhood years (115).

Several factors are important to the family's successful experiences in shaping meaningful partnerships: the effective use of parenting skills; access to quality life-support resources (health care, housing, jobs, education, recreation, safety, and other resources); involvement in building close relationships with friends and relatives; and a host of opportunities to form partnerships with the formal social systems in the community (15, 40, 68). The importance of each of these factors is briefly explored.

Researchers have only recently begun the serious task of exploring the "parent as leader" dimension of parenting and family life. The absence of sensitive caregiving in many families (e.g., in the case of Geraldine described earlier) has pointed to the need for articulating and supporting parents in the development of skills that promote growth in them and in their children (115). Galinsky (37) appropriately focuses on the interactive nature of children's and parents' growth during the early childhood years. Parents who bring to their new status of parenting/family life the leadership skills of optimism, proactive living, responsive listening, nurturing, problem solving, and "visioning" are more likely to create and sustain positive living patterns (115). Indeed, it is through the application of these skills that parents enjoin children in exploring the most intimate of human partnerships— the parent-child bond (9).

The role that informal, yet intimate, adult friends and relatives play in the shaping of parent and child relationships is of considerable importance (37, 41, 67, 77). Significant evidence has emerged to trace the critical lines of the interrelationships between supportive physical and psychological behaviors and family wellness (100, 102). Consider, for example, the observations that mothers of newborns who have highly supportive and resourceful spouses tend to engage in attachment relationships with infants much more intensively than do mothers who lack this support element (64, 85). Further, such nurturing between spouses has a very positive influence on the formation of early family bonds and spiritually rich contexts (47). This intimate partnership serves as the family's growth center that is further enriched as close relatives and friends enter the picture as extended supports.

Parents themselves point to two, three, or four adult intimates who have had a significant impact on their family's well-being (37, 60). These intimates vary in their role identity (parents, grandparents, cousins, friends) and yet have some common relationship roles with the family—emotional support, extended helping, information accessing, responsive listening, and "buffering" for dealing with the intricacies of the world beyond the family (77). Beyond these close intimates are various other informal friends who provide many sources of strength for parents. These helpers (friends at work, church, neighborhood) often provide a buffer for parents with regard to the many new situations that they confront in different stages of life.

From the very outset, parents *need to be a part of a human learning and development team* that is inclusive of their informal support network as well as of the more formalized services such as health care, child care, church and civic agencies, education, and related social service resources (86). For example, Raphael's mother was noticeably lacking in connections to these services, both in the formal and informal sense. Without such support structures, parents face an impossible task in trying to nurture children without the needed resources. Pence (86) found distinct and strong relationships between low-resource family contexts and the emergence of various negative indicators in parents and children. Garbarino (41) also notes the complex interaction of family ecology as related to needed resources and relationships during the early childhood years. Beyond the need for strong family relationships during the early years is the need for the development of strong partnerships with people and resources that enable parents and children to grow in positive and meaningful ways (77). Two examples help to focus on this concept of family-society partnerships as they are initially experienced during the early childhood years.

Ellen is a new mother, proud of her new son and eager to be a good parent. Even before the baby was born she and her husband were busy preparing the baby's room, taking a parenting course, and preparing for changes in their lives.Ellen had made arrangements to take a leave of absence for one year from her teaching position and she and her husband have spent many hours discussing how they could adjust things to help them and the baby have a good beginning.

Yet Ellen knew she was going to need many new helpers as her parents and relatives lived quite a distance away from her. In addition, her husband's work took him away frequently during the week. As Ellen embarked on her journey of parenting, she formed many friendships at church, with the pediatric nurse, and with people she had met during the parenting class. Her husband was very supportive and seemed to thrive on being a father. There were many new adjustments yet friends and helpers made Ellen feel secure in being a parent.

Nagi is the father of two young children; Len is two and Biaje is three. Nagi is a single-parent father with full custody of the children. His mother and the Head Start program have been his major supports. Nagi is very sensitive and has had a problem with alcohol. He is in counseling and is making progress in resolving his problem. He has also experienced periodic unemployment but is in a training program on heavy equipment operation. Both of the children spend their days at the Head Start program and their grandmother cares for them in the evening until Nagi gets home. Grandmother has made a big difference in the family's life, making sure the children get regular health care, that Nagi stays in counseling, keeping the children on a regular schedule, and encouraging Nagi to "get back in the church."

Two very different young families and yet the concept of partnerships is central to the well-being of both families. A supportive spouse, helpful mother, responsive child-care teacher, sensitive counselor, and/or an encouraging pediatric nurse can make a signficant difference in the lives of these young parents and their children.

The responsive and nurturing relationships that parents engage in with themselves and with other significant adults during the early years set the pattern for their potential involvement styles, facilitating or impeding the family's life-span development (66). Patterns established early on by parents serve as their foundation for continuing partnerships with caregivers, teachers, pastors, friends and, indeed, their children. It is in these various partnerships that families find sources of strength for growing and becoming contributing members of their communities. In effect, the origins of strong family-environment partnerships are in the family's early relationships. In a very real sense, the family's "social clock" and the individual's "psychological clock" are strongly influenced by the social support structures established during these early years. At the center of the family's social support structures is their approach to establishing and refining human partnerships (66). The source of strong teacher-parent partnerships is found in the microcosm of the family's early relationships.

Chapter 2

LEARNING ABOUT PARTNERSHIPS THROUGH FAMILIES

The most signficant and pervasive learning children and their parents ever encounter occurs within the family during the period from birth to six years of age of the first child (60, 129). It is during this formative period of family life that many learning attributes are acquired and internalized for use and refinement throughout the life span (24, 67, 101). Development of attitudes, beliefs, and behaviors by parents and children takes place in many different contexts that have their common identity in *family* (7). These various contexts include actions and relationships that ultimately comprise the substance of how children and parents approach their individual growth within the family, and later, in their interactions with other social settings (24, 35, 101). Four aspects of the family's role and power in influencing children's early development and learning are explored: (a) the signficance of the family's power in early learning; (b) the meaning of the many dimensions of "family"; (c) the behaviors and attributes of healthy families that promote a partnership approach to living; and (d) the role of family-community partnerships in shaping healthy contexts for early learning and development.

SIGNIFICANCE OF FAMILIES

Ironically, the power of family as experienced during the early years is often seen in the absence or distortion of the critical relationships that comprise this system (115, 127). For example, observations on the parent-infant attachment process have noted the dramatic negative influence that the lack of, or distortion of,

16

this process has had on the development of both the child and the parent (35, 43, 72, 103). Some of the outcomes such as maternal psychosis, infant weight loss, and extreme tension in the parent-infant relationship have also been related to other family dysfunctions such as alcoholism, abuse syndromes, and multiple family pathologies (14, 43, 115). It appears that the lack of healthy family dynamics not only impedes the child's development and learning but also erodes the integrity of parents even before they have had a chance to establish the family's identity in a proactive sense (12, 14, 127).

With so much energy focused on the family's problems, little attention is given to the child's learning needs such as sharing family rituals or responding to the child's learning initiatives. As Swick states:

> Ineffective families do not see themselves as in control of their lives. They tend to be unhappy, exhibit a low stress threshold, and focus on family problems more so than on family strengths. (115, p. 95)

This sense of powerlessness can become pervasive and influence the overall functioning of family members. Researchers have related individual characteristics such as low self-image, lack of self-control, and lack of direction to dysfunctional family arrangements (14, 35, 118). For example, Schaefer (104) found distinct relationships between parental beliefs about child-rearing and children's performance on cognitive and language tasks. Children of parents who placed a priority on rigid adherence to narrowly defined ways of functioning were less inquisitive than children whose parents encouraged explorative play. Sigel (108) also found relationships between parental beliefs that focused on punitive child care and inadequate cognitive functioning in children.

Just as important as cognitive development is the influence that parental and family processes have on children's socioemotional learning. For example, abused children tend to

17

be less responsive to nurturing initiatives and have more difficulty functioning effectively in social groups (43, 72, 100). They function less effectively in school, appear to suffer from persistent insecurities, and are often prone to respond in cycles of passive-aggressive behaviors (35). Wallerstein and Blakeslee (127) have found a similar process at work in families where divorce or separation was intensely bitter or abusive. The children in these contexts seem to suffer from emotional turmoil that erodes their trust in human relationships and often destroys their self-confidence.

Everyone in the family is influenced by the "power" of family living. Parental work habits, children's school performance, and intrafamily relationships are affected by the family's actions (115)—for example, there is more work disruption among adults who are experiencing severe family turmoil (14, 41). Children experiencing pervasive and intensive family stress exhibit multiple symptoms such as inattentiveness, lack of interest, poor appetite, more than usual illness, and a lack of motivation to achieve (12, 115). Marital harmony is also influenced by family events. For example, Duval (24) noted that even normal developmental changes such as entry into school for the first child disrupts the nesting habits of the family, especially the marital dyad. More serious stressors such as mother-child emotional conflicts can indirectly have a negative influence on the marriage dynamics (60, 127).

The family's power is in its identity as that process evolves through the many interactions of family members during the early childhood years. Beginning with the parents' beliefs and actions, and extending outward through parent-child and then family-community transactions, a context is developed that serves as our most intense learning arena. So far-reaching is the power of the family that recent studies of social deviance in adults have related patterns of behavior found in delinquent and adult criminals to the socioemotional attributes they developed in the family during early childhood (130). Magid and McKelvey (72),

18

for example, take note of the lack of attachment and trust-building qualities that are prevalent in adults who suffer from antisocial personality disorder. They state:

> The disease of unattachment gives rise to a broad range of psychopathy and personality disorders, including APD. In studies conducted about such patients' histories there usually appears a pattern of no significant human ties. Can such a child be reared in his own family? Unfortunately the answer is yes. The family may have few connections; the child may be unwanted, neglected, and sometimes abused. (72, p. 65)

In a similar manner, Wilson and Herrnstein (130), in reviewing several studies on "career criminals," point to severe family dysfunction during the person's early life as highly influential in the acquisition of antisocial behaviors and attributes. Fraiberg (35) found similar evidence of early family dysfunction and later adult social deviance. The most degrading process that occurs in families where nurturing and sustenance are replaced by abuse and distrust is the destruction of the child's sense of "I" and the degradation of the adult parents' sense of being a contributing and growing person (9). It appears that as this process of dysfunction forms in the family's early stage of development, it gains momentum (if left unchecked) and a series of risk behaviors and indicators emerge to enclose the family system in a negative cycle of degrading experiences (14, 63). Burchard and Burchard (12), in reviewing a longitudinal study of delinquent behavior, reference parent absence and family dysfunction during the early childhood years as major contributors to delinquency syndromes.

Family life also has the potential to influence the development and learning of children and parents in positive ways (115). A "thriving" syndrome occurs in infants who experience nurturance and attachment (9, 47, 64). Various signals emerge that are indicative of this early socioemotional health: weight gains, mutually responsive and warm parent-child interactions, and distinct progress in motor, physical, and cognitive development (35). Toddlers and young children who experience the continuity and richness of early family life enter into playful experiences more often and with more ease, initiate more inquiries about the world around them, give evidence of the rapid development of oral language, and engage in many actions that symbolize healthy differentiation as unique persons (45, 47, 66, 101).

Parents also benefit signficantly from harmonious family life during the early childhood years (37, 60). Parental histories naturally influence their approach to early family development. Given a history of adequate development in their own personal lives, for example, fathers appear to gain emotional and spiritual strength as they enter into fatherhood (85). They report a closeness to their wives and children that is indicative of a strong nurturing capacity not traditionally equated with men. It is worth noting that fathers are more likely to experience this growth in family settings where they have been valued as important partners in past marital and family relationships (47, 60). Further, the "nurturing father syndrome" is more likely to emerge in social contexts where supports exist that enable fathers to actualize their nurturing capacities (66, 73). Mothers experience similar growth during this time of family development, often reporting a signficant increase in their marital happiness as well as in the strengthening of their nurturance roles through responsive relationships with the people in their lives (60). A strong support system is integral to this parental growth during the early years of family life.

There are long-term benefits of the positive family experiences that happen during the early childhood years (115). It appears that the security, warmth, and harmony that emerge in parent-child relationships serve to support in parents and in children involvement patterns that are likely to become habits that are used throughout the life span (66). For example, Schaefer (104) found that mothers who were highly involved with their infants were also very involved in the children's lives when they were in kindergarten. In effect, the bonds formed early in infancy—and early in the mother's development—appear to be the partnership behaviors that are later extended to school and community involvement (61, 101). Other studies have found that similar long-term parent involvement behaviors have their origins in healthy family relationships during the early childhood years (108, 110). Children apparently model this trait as they develop, exhibiting more partnership behaviors in the home, with their friends, at school, and indeed throughout the life span (10, 45, 66).

Observations of developing families indicate that high-involvement patterns within the family nurture the process of individual growth (12, 52, 66). The sharing and supporting behaviors that occur within positive family relationships on a continuing basis nurture each family member to more fully develop his/her identity (9). This process appears to be lifelong, with family members differentiating through the development of their individual talents. Successful musicians, scholars, artists, and indeed, successful parents, often point to the family's supportive influence on their development (10). Longitudinal and cross-generational studies of talented children and adults point to the intensive presence of family (especially parents) in the helping and guiding processes that appear to promote individuation (10, 61, 66).

There is also more unity and more warmth behaviors in people who experience a positive family presence (100). Family as well as community interactions are often closer, more pervasive, and intensive among individuals who have experienced this closeness in family life (100). Nurturance, sensitivity, responsiveness, and warmth are qualities that are formed and sustained within an intergenerational context (101). The early childhood years are the center of this humanization process that is then refined and extended to include friendships, marriages, work relations, and innumerable other social and affective situations (66). Rossi and Rossi (101) summarize the powerful influence of early family life on human development, especially with regard to the intergenerational ties that comprise our continuing identity.

> The cohesiveness of the early family and the quality of the emotional bond between parent and child earlier on show continuing direct effects on the frequency of contact and extensiveness of the help exchanged between the generations. Although both parents and adult children may rise to occasions of great need in each other's lives, they do so with more or less grace and frequency, as a function in part of the quality of the early years of life when their lives were intimately intertwined. Each generation, then, carries its personal family history forward in time, and our understanding of the relationships between them is enriched by the knowledge of their shared past. (101, p. 458)

THE DIMENSIONS OF FAMILY

What is this entity called *family* that has such a pervasive and dynamic influence on the life of every human being? Our identities, orientation toward others, and eventually "our families" are all linked to this context (66). An assessment of the multiple meanings of the concept of family, the variations of family systems, and the key roles the family plays in influencing people's approach to life is helpful in gaining an understanding of how parents and children acquire their concepts of relating to themselves and to others. This understanding of how families form their concept of relationships is critical to having meaningful partnerships with them (115).

While emphasis often has been placed on the culture's predominant understanding of what family means, this perspective is indeed limited. For example, a survey of dictionaries will show at least fifteen different meanings, all of which are an attempt to accommodate varying value systems. The U.S. Bureau of the Census, attempting to define family broadly, settles for "two or more persons living together and related by blood, marriage, or adoption" (89, p. 2). Social scientists place the emphasis on the domestic functions families perform. Particular interest groups see it as a part of their ideology or even as an element of theology. Each of these perspectives, as well as those of others, are grounded in the culturally diverse society in which we live (89).

Integral to all of these perspectives are the unique attributes that comprise a family, regardless of the varying structures: the meeting of basic needs, some form of help-exchange system, and some means of acquiring skills for living (67). Within the transactions that families carry out to actualize these functions are the human relationships that most people identify as their concept of family (115). It is through the relationships that parents and children experience in meeting basic needs, acquiring educational skills, and maintaining the group's well-being that a concept of family is arrived at. It is through these relationships that children and parents articulate their way of relating to each other and to the larger social contexts (41).

There are various family structures in which people carry out their ways of relating and responding to the needs and challenges of life. The number of adults and children living in the system will vary and the patterns of relationships among the adults and children are indeed many. From two-parent systems to single adoptive-parent families, the combinations of parent-child and/or adult-child dyads (and triads) are endless. What happens within these various systems is also diverse. For example, in some systems, abuse of family members is common, while in others a highly nurturing environment prevails. Some families are matriarchal while others are patriarchal (67, 89).

The common element in these varying family arrangements is the influence they have on how people develop their concept of relating to themselves and to others. Considerable evidence suggests that *parents and children carry forward the concept of relationships acquired in the family to other social contexts*

23

(9, 66). Family researchers have identified several relationship processes that are heavily influenced by early family life: development of roles; acquisition of help-exchange skills; formation of trust; development of a sense of closeness; acquisition of problem-solving skills; and a proclivity toward responsive listening. Each of these processes is vital to the relationship-building process. In one dimension or another, they occur within all families.

FAMILY RELATIONSHIPS
AS FOUNDATION FOR PARTNERSHIPS

Families, like all living systems, must interact with other systems if they are to grow in positive ways. It is through social networks, relationships with formal support services, and partnerships with caregivers, teachers, pastors, and other helpers that families acquire the resources and support essential to their continuing growth (40, 41, 60, 68, 77, 86). Learning to develop effective family-environment relationships is a continuing process that requires skills and attitudes that promote recriprocal and responsive interactions (11, 63). These skills and attitudes include the social and cognitive tools that parents and children initially develop within their relationships. For example, trust is essential to any viable relationship; it is initially developed in the parent-child attachment process and within the family's many bonding rituals (9, 35, 66). Likewise, truly effective partnerships require the partners (such as parents and teachers) to carry out multiple roles in a flexible manner. Both skills—trust and flexibility—are learned during the family's early, formative period (24, 37, 60).

Eight relationship/partnership-building processes that are used throughout the life span have their foundation in the early childhood years: role flexibility, trust development, help-exchange, responsive listening, individuation, group-functioning skills, nurturance, and problem-solving (115). Individuals who

24

never fully develop these skills are more likely to experience difficulties in relationship/partnership contexts. For example, the child who is unable to develop a trusting relationship with the teacher is likely to avoid meaningful involvements in the classroom. The substance and importance of each of these process-skills is briefly explored with regard to the partnership-building process.

Trust is the foundation upon which all significant relationships are developed (9). It is a dynamic process that is based on a faith that other significant people will respond in consistent, loving, and responsive ways. It is a learned process that is acquired during the early childhood years and continually refined over the life span. To trust someone is not to give the person full reign but rather to see him/her as a growing individual who is sensitive and responsive to the needs of others in a consistently humane manner (35, 47, 63, 129). Our first experiences with trust are embedded in the parent-child attachment process. However, it is the various warm and responsive experiences we have with intimate others over the life span that enables us to generate a trusting orientation toward life (9, 129). All meaningful partnerships are based on trust. A parent or teacher unable to carry out trusting behaviors with others is certain to experience severe problems in teacher-parent partnerships (66).

Any viable partnership requires of the participants the skill of *role flexibility*. Inclusive of this skill, for example, is the ability to nurture as well as to be nurtured; to lead as well as to follow; to be supportive as well as to receive support (63, 110). In effect, good partners are able to see the various dimensions of a relationship, and then act to promote the well-being of eveyone involved. A good example of role flexibility is seen in the early family relationships where fathers become the key supporters of new mothers, carrying out roles that both nurture and sustain the mother while she is centering her energy on the infant (85). Role flexibility provides partnerships with perspective-taking, which is essential to effective problem solving (41). For example, it has been found (117) that parents who became involved in multiple school-home involvement activities were more likely to see the teacher's role in a broader perspective. Likewise, children who observe and experience family relationships where adults carry out different roles in a supportive manner tend to internalize this orientation in their interactions with others (100, 108).

Help-exchange is common to all healthy relationships (110); this process is actually what makes partnerships possible and meaningful. It is a dynamic process that is initially seen in the mother-infant relationship, where infants receive intensive support from mothers and where mothers receive their primary psychological and spiritual source of identity as caregivers (66). A truly authentic relationship does not view help-exchange as bartering but rather as the means by which both individual and group needs are sustained in a responsive manner (60). In this sense, the physical help exchanged in relationships is simply a surface indicator of a deeper spiritual exchange that speaks of a reciprocal commitment of the individuals to each other's growth and well-being (37). For example, the father who changes his schedule to be more available to the family is indeed modeling the essence of the real meaning of help-exchange. This process-skill is vital to viable family-school relationships because it serves as the source of power by which parents, children, and teachers help each other grow and learn (113).

Responsive listening is integral to the growth-oriented relationships that occur in families and schools. The beauty of parent-child caring scenes is in the nonverbal yet intimate responsiveness of a group of people to the mutual well-being of each person. It is through the many family experiences where individuals change and respond to each others' growth needs that children and parents acquire true listening skills. Many families wisely set aside times to promote this listening skill, thus assuring that their relationships are not impeded by the spiritual void that can emerge when no one is listening (9). Later, parents and children will be called upon to apply this skill in their many relationships with teachers and other helpers. Perspective-taking, a skill necessary for developing mutuality in relationships, is best actualized through responsive listening (115).

A hallmark of the different stages of human development is the process of *individuation* (24, 35, 43, 47, 66). In other words, with the growth process should come an increasingly sophisticated person who is differentiating him/herself to a marked degree. This process gains its momentum during the early childhood years, especially as it is carried out within the fabric of the family's socioemotional and spiritual relationships (66). In supportive families, for example, two-year-olds begin to individuate and take on personality traits that define them as unique and distinct persons within the family. Parents also are continuously developing themselves through internalizing new roles and refining old ones (37). Strong and consistent relationships require that the participants have this sense of individuation. In dysfunctional relationships, for example, a member(s) of the family may not be differentiating and developing a sense of individual identity, often because others in the family either are lacking in a functional identity or are restricted by a very limited concept of who they are as individuals (14). Yet healthy family-environment interactions require that parents and children master the oneness-differentiation process so that they can extend themselves successfully into other relationships (37, 63).

Secure, developing individuals can enter into productive relationships successfully. Part of this security is acquired through learning the give-and-take of *group functioning skills* that are, or should be, acquired during the family's early experiences (63). We learn these skills best in settings that allow us to find supportive ways of relating to a few people at first, and then expanding our reach to larger groups. This process-skill is inclusive of the many other relationship skills explored here, e.g., listening, help-exchange, and trust development. It is a process seen early in the family's development where rituals are established and used to build a cohesive sense of identity. Learning to value, then develop, and ultimately, to support group cohesiveness is a lifelong process with deep and strong roots in the family's early life experiences (101). Multiple exchanges such as compromising on individual goals and schedules among parents, and alternating roles, which parents and children will do for a lifetime, are the substance of what families use to build these group-functioning skills. In today's society, parents and children extend and refine these skills in their partnerships in child care, health care, informal social networks, and in many other contexts (77).

Two relationship-building skills that sustain and enrich all human partnerships are *nurturance* and *problem solving*, both of which have their origins in the family's early relationships (110). Considerable research has shown that nurturance (providing self and others with support, a sense of uniqueness, and resources) is the continuing energy source for all human relationships, especially relationships that require intensive and sustaining involvement such as parenting and teaching (38). The family itself, especially during the early childhood years, requires significant nurturing in order to form lasting relationships (41, 63, 77, 101). The psychological and spiritual dimensions of this caring process are the foundations of the nurturing behaviors that parents and children use to strengthen their relationships (9).

Problem solving is another skill that emerges in healthy families as they find formal and informal ways of resolving the stressors in their lives. Whether these stressors are developmental or biological, the means by which parents and children resolve them become their way of relating to other issues that arise in their community interactions (110). The most graphic and negative evidence on this extension of one's problem-solving approach is found in the cycle of abusive behavior. A tendency toward dysfunctional coping has been observed in adults who were abused as children (43). Similar observations have been noted in the correspondence between children's school behavior and the problem-solving dynamics in their families (63).

Clearly, the early relationship-building experiences of parents and children establish a style by which they negotiate their transactions in-and-beyond the family. This schema includes the individual's perceptions regarding her/his own value, uniqueness, and abilities as well as her/his orientation toward relating to others. Ultimately, we extend our relationship-building skills to the many partnerships we have with others, including teachers and other helpers (110).

FAMILY ATTRIBUTES
THAT PROMOTE PARTNERSHIPS

Healthy families utilize the relationship-building process to develop an environment in which positive living can flourish (110). Family researchers have identified ten attributes of families who seem to function in healthy modes: love, religiosity, respect, communication, individuality, togetherness, consideration, commitment, parental competence, and sharing (110, 115). Each attribute is briefly reviewed as it has been related to the involvement of parents and children in building meaningful partnerships.

Love

Strong emotional bonds are present in various family relationships, beginning with parental attachment to infants and permeating their later socioemotional growth. This intensive caring serves as the family's foundation for valuing each person's individual growth (9, 35, 110).

Religiosity

Early family rituals promote a strong sense of faith through parent-parent and parent-child behaviors that characterize the accepting, valuing, and nurturing of each family member. This sense of faith serves as the family's unifying force

29

with regard to life's meaning. It is actualized through actual behaviors and through religious and spiritual symbols (9, 110).

Respect

The presence of helping and responsive actions gives a clear sense of mutuality within family relationships. Family members show their concern for each other; a beginning point of this caring is often seen in marital or friendship partnerships. This concern for each person's integrity is also seen in the family's approach to supporting each person's well-being (63, 110).

Communication

Visible signs of an active responsive-listening philosophy are present: changing work schedules, listening to each other's problems, supporting projects of other family members, allowing for growth in each other's individual lives, and responding to the family's common needs. Understandably, family communication behaviors are critical to their continued growth, both within the family's interactions and in their partnerships with others in the community (110).

Individuality

Each person in the family is seen as unique and encouraged to differentiate in terms of their interests and talents. Family members take pride in each other's individual accomplishments and support each person in their attempts to grow. This attribute of promoting individuation within the family is extended to other relationships such as in parent-teacher partnership (9, 110).

Togetherness

Just as the individual is highly valued, there is also a clear sense of working together as a team. People share in carrying out roles to meet the family's needs. A sense of supportiveness is present as seen in activities where the family is truly valued. Later, this same philosophy is carried forward into various community involvement efforts (66, 110).

Consideration

The needs and feelings of family members are considered among its individual members. Sensitive actions are observed as family members interact with each other, responding with compassion to the problems different individuals confront. This attribute of consideration is also seen in the family's involvement with others in the community who are in need (67, 110, 115).

Commitment

A sense of long-term support is present in the family—a willingness to work through problems no matter how difficult they might be. The sense of optimism and strength that emerge from this true commitment is vital to the family's internal security as well as to their relationships in external settings such as the school. This attribute is often seen in the later behavior of children and parents as they engage in supportive activities in the school and the community (110, 115).

Sharing

A helping network in which family members share resources, responsibilities, ideas, and feelings is prevalent. A sense of teamwork is evident in carrying out family tasks. As this attribute develops, families have an essential skill for becoming partners in school and community activities (110, 115).

Parental Competence

Providing the family with leadership, nurturing parents provide children with guidance and support the family in dealing with developmental and environmental changes. Parents exhibit an understanding of child and family development and of their place in providing the guidance for both individual and family

31

development. A particularly relevant skill in competent parents is their ability to assist the family in forming viable linkages in the community (24, 37, 68, 115).

These attributes, as observed in healthy and maturing families, are developmental in nature, with the foundation taking shape during the early childhood years and extensions and refinements taking place within the family's growth. Families do not carry out these attributes in a static manner, but rather engage in multiple experiences in ways that support the continuing development of these characteristics (110). The relationship-building skills and attributes described provide families with the tools and the meaning essential for having positive and growing partnerships with schools and other social systems. Parents, as research clearly shows, provide the leadership in this growth process (115).

Chapter 3

PARENTS AND TEACHERS: THE LEADERSHIP TEAM

As families develop, they must have sources of growth beyond their immediate boundaries. Beginning in infancy, parents and children develop a support system and partnerships with each other and their helpers (9). One of the hallmarks of dysfunctional families is their inability to create some control and direction in their relationships with each other and with the needed resources in their environment (63). Swick notes that—

> Healthy families appear to gain access to needed supports and develop skills for utilizing resources in a productive mode. It is not that healthy families never experience high stress, it is the way they use the environment and their skills in responding to it effectively. (115, p. 10)

The effective use of resources and providing linkages to social contexts that support family growth are leadership skills that parents use throughout the family's development. In their relationships with teachers, parents must carry out several roles, all of which depend on their skills for entering into and developing meaningful partnerships (11, 68).

Likewise, teachers of young children have a major leadership role not only in guiding children's development and learning but also in designing and implementing arrangements that promote continuity between family and school experiences (98, 114). Powell (92) notes that any extreme disparity between the goals of parents and teachers during the early childhood years reduces the meaning of family-school relationships and impedes everyone's efforts at finding success in learning. In effect, parents and teachers are in leadership roles as they attempt to create partnerships that strengthen children's school success and enrich their own personal growth (114). Research has identified attributes and roles that parents and teachers use to build successful partnerships (44, 97, 114). An understanding of these attributes and roles provides insight into how to develop effective partnerships. For example, understanding that parental self-image is essential to successful teacher-parent partnerships can lead to the integration of this need in parent involvement programs (44). Further, teacher sensitivity to the key attributes that they should pursue should strengthen their understanding of the dynamic roles they play in providing parent-involvement leadership (114).

PARENT ATTRIBUTES
THAT PROMOTE PARTNERSHIPS

Observations of parents who are successful in establishing and nurturing meaningful partnerships with teachers indicate that they have acquired several attributes (114). Warmth, sensitivity, nurturance, listening, and consistency are personality attributes that have been noted (15). Some additional attributes noted include marital happiness, family harmony, success in prior collaborative experiences, and an openness to the ideas of others (114). Parent efficacy (a sense of optimism and self-direction) contributes to strong teacher-parent relationships. This sense of efficacy is related to a series of attributes. Four attribute categories comprise parents' system of integrity: self-image, control of self, one's developmental orientation, and interpersonal involvements (115). While various strategies are included in later sections, an example of how teachers might engage parents in seeing these roles as important to their family's development is included here for each attribute.

Parent Self-Image

How parents view themselves is related to all of their actions, especially with regard to their motivation for being involved in supporting the family's growth through community and school partnerships (44). Parents who have a positive self-image tend to see their children in a more meaningful sense, to spend more time with them in learning activities, and to have a more positive attitude toward teachers and the educational process (46). Early childhood programs, especially parent education efforts, have found that involving parents in meaningful learning experiences with their children during the preschool years strengthens children's and parents' self-image and is influential in helping parents and teachers build strong partnerships (44, 91, 115).

Parent Self-Image Strategy

Have parents identify something they like about themselves. Have them share these things with other parents in small groups. In the larger group, have parents share how they felt when others took pride in their positive sense of self.

Parent Efficacy

Parent efficacy (control over one's relationships and actions) is also highly related to having successful partnerships with individuals and groups beyond the family (115). Schaefer's work (104) on parents' locus of control is instructive in this regard. He found that parents who exhibited a high internal locus of control during the early period of the child's life were indeed still highly involved with their children (and the teacher) in kindergarten and first grade. He found a correspondence between the parents' sense of mastery over their environment and their actions as related to the child's well-being. Parents involved in intensive early childhood parent education programs appear to gain in their sense of efficacy and extend this power into their involvement with teachers well into the primary grades (104, 115, 117).

35

Parent Efficacy Strategy

Put parents into learning teams and have them solve a problem together. Have them identify the skills they used to solve the problem. How did they feel about their working together as a team? Now, have them discuss ways that they can use the same skills in their personal lives.

Parent Development

Parent-teacher relationships take on more meaning when parents are achieving growth through intentional development and maturation (37, 72). The developmental gains parents acquire through the maturation process, which is indeed an intentional endeavor, provide them with "perspective-taking"— a skill that is integral to working with others in productive ways (68). Negotiating the marital, friendship, and family challenges that arise in the early years of family development successfully adds a new dimension to parents' perspectives about their development, one that strengthens their attitudes and skills for relating to new challenges (37). Gordon (44), Fraiberg (35), and Stinnett (111) have noted the congruence between successful parent development and high, positive parent/family involvement with their support systems.

Parent Development Strategy

Have new parents share with other parents ways that they adjusted to the first few months of parenting. Have experienced parents identify successful experiences they have had in being a parent. Have both groups discuss (in small groups) how these successful experiences helped them to become more mature and effective in both personal and parental roles.

Parent Interpersonal Skills

Indeed, parents need strong, reciprocal relationships with support groups such as teachers. During parents' early development, supportive relationships strengthen their position to grow and gain self-confidence in their leadership abilities. In turn, such parents develop the attributes of mutuality and supportiveness in assisting others in their growth roles (9). Parents who lack support are isolated from meaningful community resources and often fear having close relationships beyond the family (41, 43).

Interpersonal Skills Strategy

Have parents identify the "key people" other than their spouse who have helped them meet the various challenges of life. Ask them why these people were so important to them. In what ways were these people helpful to them?

In combination, the four attributes that comprise parents' system of integrity enable them to carry out beneficial exchanges within the family and with their supportive persons such as teachers. Emerging from this foundation are additional parent attributes that have been observed to contribute to strong teacher-parent relationships: a continuing involvement in personal development experiences, a history of successful relationships with church and civic activities, a responsiveness to the needs of others, an inquisitive orientation, a sense of optimism about life, and a continuing involvement in family literacy activities during the early childhood years (115).

Teacher reports on the qualities of highly involved parents correspond with the portrait of persons who have had success in developing healthy family relationships and in building positive linkages with the community. In reports on parent-involvement attributes cited by teachers, the following points have been emphasized: positive parental self-image, maturity, family harmony, optimism, responsiveness and follow-through on teacher requests, and active support of the teacher were attributes of highly involved parents (30, 92, 117). *It is important to note that these attributes were observed among parents of various socioeconomic and ethnic backgrounds.*

In a recent study of the involvement patterns of at-risk parents, it was noted that parental beliefs regarding learning, the availability of a strong support system, positive self-image, and healthy family relationships were observed in highly involved parents (121). It was also noted that as parents acquired information on how to help their children with school-related tasks, many attributes such as positive attitudes toward the school and a responsiveness to teacher requests surfaced in parents who at first seemed uninterested in partnership activities. Further, this same study found that when schools provided supports such as transportation, child care, flexible conference schedules, and home-based activities, parent involvement among at-risk parents increased dramatically (121).

Two insights emerge for teachers of young children with regard to encouraging the development of attributes that promote partnership skills in parents: it is important to carry out community and school strategies that promote the development of these attributes in parents during their earliest parenting endeavors, and to create parent-involvement designs that include supportive and flexible arrangements that truly invite parents to become partners in their children's education (92, 121).

Teacher support as well as total community involvement of parents involved in developing relationship-building attributes must recognize the wide variations in how parents actualize these skills within different cultural, ethnic, racial, and individualized contexts (34, 91, 92). Cultural factors and/or conditions that place parents at risk may influence parents toward more passive roles with regard to being involved in decision making. This in no way reflects parents' lack of interest but may indicate their strong belief (or low self-esteem) that teachers are the sole decision makers on classroom procedures or curriculum issues (34). Thus, an invitational approach that assures parents that their involvement in shared decision making is being encouraged will be needed to alleviate parental fears of encroaching on areas of teacher dominance.

Finally, it is helpful to recognize that parents arrive at points of development related to these different attributes in various ways and at different times in their lives (37). Some parents who have more access to integrity–building experiences are more secure in close partnerships; others may withdraw in the wake of such challenges (118). For example, first-time parents may need more confidence-building and parents who are in at-risk situations surely need high levels of support. The work of Gordon (44), Schaefer (104), Swick (115), and Powell (91) points to the success that can be achieved when the empowerment attributes parents need are recognized and integrated into teachers' partnership efforts.

TEACHER ATTRIBUTES
THAT PROMOTE PARTNERSHIPS

Throughout history teachers have been encouraged to view their role as encompassing a partnership with parents. Considerable theory and research have supported this perspective (44, 92). Indeed, most early childhood teacher education programs include some coursework and practical experience on parent involvement. There is research that notes particular personal attributes of teachers that strengthen their position in establishing positive relationships with parents and children. For example, it has been noted that the warmth dimension (the caring and receptivity that occur in meaningful interactions) increases the likelihood of having productive relationships (6, 20, 100). Openness, a personality factor often cited as related to positive human relationships, has been correlated with teacher support of children and parents (108).

Four personal attributes of teachers that enhance their involvement with parents during the early childhood years are *sensitivity, flexibility, reliability,* and *accessibility.* Sensitive teachers take an interest in the personal dynamics of the family in a positive way, giving consideration to unique problems or concerns and responding to them in a compassionate manner

(39). An extension of this attribute is teachers' openness (accessibility) to parents' ideas on their children's development and learning. Even when a teacher is unable to carry out a parent request, the responsive listening of the teacher to parent ideas increases the value of their relationship (93). Consistent and reliable performance by teachers on important family-school issues such as communication, positive discipline, child well-being, family involvement, and effective teaching have been noted as behaviors that parents indicate as being highly desirable in teachers (115). An attribute that increases the trust level between teachers and parents is flexibility—the willingness to adapt to particular child and parent needs (122).

From the perspective of parents, the following character-istics are desirable in a teacher of young children: trust, warmth, closeness, positive self-image, effective classroom management, child-centeredness, knowledge of subject, continuing interaction with parents, positive discipline, nurturance, and effective teaching (94). It is evident that teachers who are in a process of continuing personal growth, are more receptive to parent involvement and actually take more initiatives to pursue the partnership process (122). It appears that teachers who are secure in their own personal growth are more likely to be sensitive and responsive to the cultural, ethnic, and individual needs of the children and parents they teach (34).

The nurturance of strong teacher-parent partnerships requires the supportive development of professional attributes that promote this process in teachers (2). Researchers (30, 31, 38, 44, 51, 59, 93, 105, 115, 126) have identified teacher attributes that are related to the successful involvement of parents: teacher attitudes, teacher initiatives to involve parents, teacher training, administrative support for parent involvement, teaching style, teaching philosophy, and involvement in professional associa-tions. Swick and McKnight (120) highlight some of the key findings with regard to the relationships between teacher attributes and the parent-teacher partnership process.

1. There is a clear relationship between teacher attitudes toward parents and the level of parent involvement activities carried out by teachers. For example, it has been found that teachers who strongly believed in extending school learning into the home also had the highest level of parent involvement activities (30, 122).

2. The initiation and development of meaningful teacher-parent relationships is a hallmark of effective teachers. Gordon (44) noted that parents identified high parent-involvement teachers as their children's most effective teachers. Epstein (30) noted this same attribute. Swick and McKnight (122) further noted that high parent-involvement teachers were experienced, members of a professional association, and were very positive toward working with parents.

3. Teacher training on parent involvement increases the actual involvement of teachers in pursuing such efforts. Ascher (2) notes the potential for increasing parent/family involvement in schools when appropriate training is provided. Rich (97) indicates this potential has been achieved to some degree through teacher training using the Home–School model. Further, it was found that early childhood-trained teachers, who typically are required to take parent/family involvement courses, exhibited a higher degree of total support for parent education and parent involvement than did teachers trained in elementary or middle school programs (122).

4. The importance of administrative support for having parent involvement activities has been advocated strongly by several researchers (2, 30, 31, 44, 114, 115). In studies where it has been assessed (122), it is clearly related to the amount of parent involvement taking place in schools. Teachers who perceive that their school administrative team is supportive of parent involvement have higher levels of contact with parents and a stronger belief system regarding the important role of parents (6, 20, 31, 122).

5. Professional association membership, teaching philosophy, and teaching style have also been related to teachers' support of parent involvement (114). Apparently the active renewal of one's professional growth that can come from participation in professional associations increases teacher interest in pursuing partnership activities with parents (122). A developmentally oriented teaching philosophy and an integrated-day teaching style also seem to correlate with more parent involvement behaviors by teachers (122).

Based on what is known regarding teacher attributes that promote parent involvement, especially during the early childhood years, it can be said with much confidence that teachers who promote strong parent-teacher partnerships strongly believe in the vital role of parents in their children's education; have engaged in specialized training related to having effective partnerships; are members of professional associations; have the support of school leaders; are generally child- and family-oriented in their philosophy and teaching style; and are more active in actually pursuing long-term, meaningful teacher-parent partnerships (115, 122).

TEACHER-PARENT PARTNERSHIP ROLES: A FRAMEWORK

Building upon their leadership skills, parents and teachers can construct viable partnerships best within a role-relationship system that supports their common efforts. At the foundation of strong partnerships is the need for teachers and parents to have an understanding of both the unique and the complementary roles that are integral to their successful endeavors. As Epstein (30) notes, extreme dissonance between parent and teacher beliefs regarding the roles that comprise their relationship can lead to serious conflicts. For example, parents may see for themselves a significant role in school decision making; yet, if teachers do not also hold this perspective, serious conflict is inevitable (109). A beginning point is to clarify what parent involvement partnerships mean to those participating in the process.

Swick (114) notes four basic levels of parental participation: *learning, supporting, doing,* and *participatory decision making.* In the learning or parent education role, parents acquire knowledge, skills, and behaviors related to increasing their parental and/or family competence (44, 91). Parental support roles take many forms but generally refer to the validity and value that parents give to the teaching/learning process as carried out by teachers (6). This typically is seen in parental value statements ("I support my child's teacher") or in surface-level support behaviors ("I'll make sure he does his homework"). In the doing role, parents become actively engaged in collaborative activities with teachers through school and home learning experiences. For example, parents may assist teachers in planning and implementing field trips or may carry out a specific home-learning activity with their children (114). At yet another level, parents and teachers join in decision making (22). In this process, parents engage in actually helping to shape goals and strategies for classroom and school improvement (2, 19).

In gaining an understanding of the levels of participation, parents and teachers need to address the degree of intensity of their mutual involvement (114). There are various ways to address this element of involvement such as using a passive-active-very active scheme (114).

Passive: Parent is minimally involved; responds mostly to urgent requests by teacher; rarely participates in learning, supporting, or doing roles.

Active: Parent is involved with teacher on a regular basis; participates in various learning, doing, and supporting roles and a few decision-making activities.

Very Active: Parent has entered into an intense partnership with the teacher; involved in key leadership roles as well as in learning, supporting, and doing roles.

43

Figure 1
Parenting Roles Within the Family

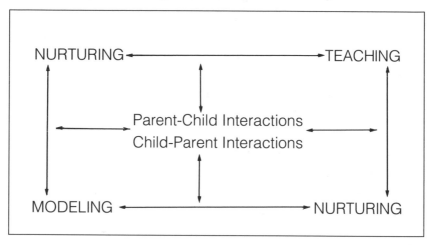

With the levels and intensity of parent involvement serving as a framework, parents and teachers can benefit from clarifying their unique and complementary roles. With regard to parent-teacher partnerships, especially during the early childhood years, the following roles have been highlighted as unique to parents with regard to two settings, the family and the school: nurturer, teacher, role model, learner, doer, supporter, and decision maker (105). The first three roles are placed in the context of the family. In this sense, the family partnership is seen as the parents' first priority: nurturing children and adults toward healthy relationships; teaching children through the natural relationships and opportunities that arise in the family; and providing children with a positive role model for living (105). Figure 1 provides a representation of the dynamics of these roles as they might be carried out by parents during the early childhood years.

In the framework of relationships presented in Figure 1, parents initiate their involvement and partnership behaviors within the family. Typically, this involvement takes on the form of nurturing relationships among parents and children, with parents modeling and teaching through the family's many natural interactions (9). It is (or should be) the predominant form of parent involvement during the family's formative period of life, usually during infancy and toddlerhood. White (129) observes that it is during this period of the family's development that children and parents acquire their repertoire of affective and social skills needed for healthy family life and for later use in functioning effectively in school and community settings. In particular, parents formalize the relationship-building skills needed for having positive family interactions and for later use in developing partnerships with their helpers (37, 66).

The four involvement roles that parents contribute to their children's education are learning, supporting, doing, and decision making. In the learning role, parents participate in various parent education experiences such as group meetings, home visits, use of specified materials (122). In supporting roles, parents carry out activities that support the teacher's efforts to achieve the best possible learning program for the children and families (113). The doing role engages parents in becoming actively involved with the teacher in implementing some aspect of the educational program, e.g., tutoring, field trips, class projects (114). Efforts that involve parents in participatory decision making with teachers usually have a common purpose of improving the school's educational program (122). Figure 2 provides a representation of school involvement roles as uniquely contributed by parents.

Figure 2
Parent Involvement Roles in School

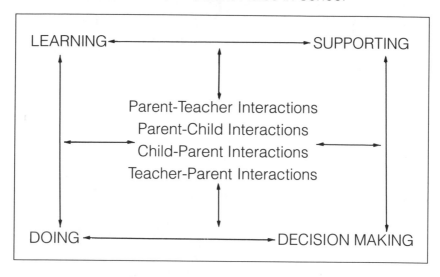

The roles that parents carry out in connection with the school evolve from the roles they initially use to develop positive family relationships. Learning, supporting, doing, and decision making are based upon the values of commitment, sharing, and growth that parents develop in their family involvement roles (122). When parents have not developed the foundation roles of nurturing, teaching, and modeling, they often experience difficulty in attempting to carry out roles such as learning, doing, supporting, and decision making (115). With the emergence of the family's earlier involvement in child care and early childhood settings, parents are engaging in these roles earlier than in the past. Today's parent is, by necessity, becoming a lifelong learner, engaged more fully in human development issues, and taking on more responsibility not only for the child's education but also for that of others in the community too (20)!

Teachers also make unique contributions to the teacher-parent partnership during the early childhood years. Family-centered roles of teachers include support, education, and guidance (104, 115). A major emphasis in teacher training programs has been on the teacher's role in parent education (15). In this role teachers utilize various strategies to provide parents with information on topics and issues related to their parenting and family development/learning. An extension of this role is the support role, in which teachers attempt to assist parents in obtaining the resources needed (health care, child care, counseling, housing) for a positive environment for the family's development (31, 40). Teachers are also informal consultants to parents, carrying out the critical role of guidance (114). In this capacity, teachers often confer with parents on a variety of issues related to the well-being of the child and family (104).

Like parents, teachers' participation in these roles varies in intensity, often depending upon their development of the attributes discussed previously and the situations in which they are teaching. Figure 3 represents the key teacher roles related to their supportive involvement with the family.

Figure 3
Teacher Involvement Roles with the Family

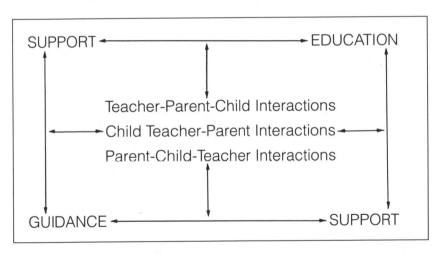

Teachers' early involvement in supporting families in their development of healthy family beginnings has increased dramatically during the past thirty years. National, state, and local policymakers are advocating increased early intervention efforts by school and community agencies that support families in acquiring the social and educational skills needed for lifelong learning (1, 19, 72, 86, 106, 126). For example, the efforts of some schools through home visitation programs offer many opportunities for teachers and caregivers to carry out support, education, and guidance activities (115).

Distinct roles that teachers use in support of parent and child involvement in the classroom include: nurturing, teaching, guiding, and decision making (114, 115). The nurturing that teachers employ with children and parents is distinctive in that it reinforces that caring life-styles begun in the home can be extended to other early childhood environments (2, 32). Teachers also carry out many support activities, providing children with validation, reaching out to parents in need, and developing mutually beneficial relationships with the family (115). Guidance is a continuing partnership role that teachers use in assisting parents and children in the growth process (39). Decision-making strategies directed toward the well-being of the children and parents in their classrooms are at the center of teacher involvement in all early learning efforts (114). Figure 4 presents the interactive system of key teacher-involvement roles.

Figure 4

Teacher Support Roles of Family Involvement in School

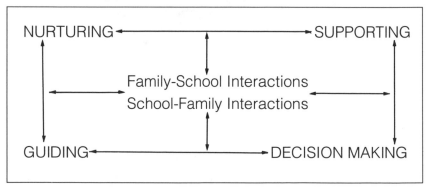

There are many situations in which teachers carry out these roles: showing their valuing of the family in their advocacy of family-support policies in the community; engaging in support activities that improve the lives of parents and children in need; providing families with guidance on making the transition from home to school; and involving families in making decisions that will promote their well-being (2, 6, 26, 92, 115).

Beyond the distinct roles that parents and teachers perform in establishing a foundation for their partnership, there are common roles that enable the partnership to materialize. These process roles provide the means by which parents and teachers can establish, nurture, and continually refine their partnership (105). These roles include: collaboration, planning, communication, and evaluation (92, 105, 114). See Figure 5 for a schemata representing the nature of these roles.

Figure 5
Teacher-Parent Collaboration Roles

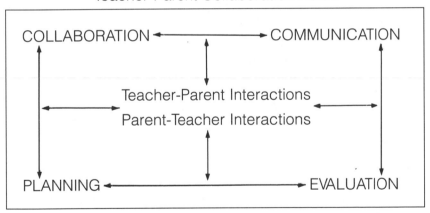

Collaboration is the core of the teacher-parent partnership process (20, 22, 30, 80, 114). It involves parents and teachers in working together on virtually all aspects of the growth process as it relates to the family-school learning ecology. It is a process by which parents expand the potential of children's environment as well as their own through continuous, planned

DISCARDED

LIBRARY
FORSYTH TECHNICAL COMMUNITY COLLEGE
2100 SILAS CREEK PARKWAY
WINSTON-SALEM, NC 27103-5197

interactions (92, 115). Joint efforts by parents and teachers in planning the various elements of their partnership, both individual and common ventures related to the learning, doing, supporting, and nurturing roles, are essential to positive and meaningful partnerships. This planning needs to occur in their individual roles such as parent-planning home-learning experiences for the family as well as in their collaborative roles such as where parents and teachers plan joint school and family learning activities (114).

The growth process is rapid and intensive in children, parents, and teachers during the early childhood years; communication is the means by which these partners support and enrich each other's growth. Examples of this communication linkage are endless: daily interactions between teacher and parent; monthly newsletters; periodic phone calls; sending home children's work samples; and regularly scheduled conferences (38). Feedback, in the form of continuing evaluation, allows the teacher-parent partnership to change as conditions, development, and needs require. It is the part of the collaboration that offers parents and teachers an opportunity to observe children's growth (and their own), to share with each other their perceptions of that growth, and to then engage in planning how best to facilitate it in both school and home settings (116).

As research and practice have provided a framework by which parents and teachers can strengthen their relationships and thus enhance children's development and learning, the deployment of early childhood school-family strategies is emerging as a major force in improving the learning and development process (31). By recognizing the need for early involvement of parents and children in successful relationships with their environment, schools and communities can organize designs for initiating and supporting meaningful parent-teacher partnerships. Through parent and teacher initiatives, the process of mutual involvement can be successfully arranged, especially as these partners carry out their unique and common roles in growing and intentional ways.

Chapter 4
DEVELOPING PARTNERSHIPS DURING THE EARLY CHILDHOOD YEARS

A starting point for the initiation of partnerships during the early childhood years is in helping parents and teachers to acquire an understanding of their roles in supporting children's development and learning as well as their own growth (38, 97, 114). This process takes many forms; it is a means by which families and schools can come to a fuller realization of how they can support each other in their attempts to become full partners in the community's development (105). Indeed, the lack of early parent involvement in developing both internal family relationships that are supportive of healthy living and external partnerships with helping professionals has contributed to confusion with regard to appropriate roles and relationships and has impeded the family's growth (86, 105). As Galinsky (38, 39) takes note, the early years are not only a very formative period for children but also are a very challenging and demanding time for parents and teachers.

INITIATING PARTNERSHIPS EARLY

Parents welcome support as they confront the many challenges of family life during the early childhood years. In addition, this period of family formation offers everyone a chance to build on the positive aspects of children's early experiences as well as a chance to shape parenting attitudes that are conducive to long-term involvement in partnership endeavors. It is during this initial part of parenthood that the core involvement behaviors of parents needed for supporting healthy family life are formed: *nurturing, teaching,* and *modeling* (105). Efforts to support this period of parenting and family life have indicated that there are some clear benefits: parents can acquire information and support on critical parenting and child/family issues; parents can engage in experiences in which they begin the development of their core parenting behaviors; parents and children can engage in early partnership behaviors with significant helpers beyond the home; and, families can alleviate or resolve at-risk situations that threaten them and can strengthen their position for having meaningful relationships with each other and with their helpers in the community (40, 44, 70).

While most schools traditionally have left these early involvements with parents to others in the community, a more collaborative system involving teachers with many other helping professionals is emerging as an effective way of enhancing children's school success (15, 20, 30, 91, 105, 114). In effect, much of the family's early learning style is formed by kindergarten. For some time effective teachers, either formally or informally, have engaged in or strongly supported these early partnership-building efforts with the family. The strategies and examples presented here focus on the early, formative years of parenting, and include practices and ideas that teachers, other school personnel, and other community agents have used to support parents in beginning life with positive and growing activities.

Initial Focus: The Parent's Development

Recent insights and efforts carried out by parent educators strongly suggest that the initial point of "relationship-building" must focus on the personal dimensions of the parents' developmental status and the related issues that will help them to be effective in both personal and parental roles (114). Powell (92) reinforces this point with his observation of parents of infants and toddlers who were engaged in group parent education sessions. He found that "kitchen talk" (informal discussion time) often centered on the personal and developmental needs of parents, so vital to their emergence as positive parents. That is, parents created an informal support group that added a new dimension to their lives. There is an important message here for teachers and other helping professionals: parents want to be validated and enriched so they can successfully entertain the complex issues of being a parent (37).

Galinsky (37), for example, advocates that initial parent learning experiences emphasize the nurturing, teaching, and modeling roles as they are formed by parents during the early childhood years. It is vital that parents reach beyond simply being comfortable with understanding the roles of parenting and seek to gain a broader sense of their personal growth as it relates to parenting. This need to "image" oneself as a caring and worthy person is emphasized by Galinsky in her work on the developmental nature of parenting. And, as she so aptly points out, this process begins (or should begin) in pregnancy and continues throughout the parent's development, both as a person and as a parent (37). Perhaps the most important image new parents (and experienced parents, for that matter) need to shape is that of themselves as nurturers (115). Far too often parents are provided materials and experiences that focus on the mechanics of birthing or the basics of parenting and that never engage them in seeking an image of themselves as loving persons.

Becoming a parent, like growing as a person, is a relationship-building process that requires one to encounter experiences where one intentionally sees oneself as caring and loving, thus prompting feelings of confidence in being a parent and in being a partner with others in this process (68, 85, 86, 100). For parents to be able to carry out the teaching and modeling roles, they must have this foundation of faith in themselves that evolves from their growth as nurturing persons (9). Indeed, exemplary early family and parenting support programs are focused on this critical element of the *parent as nurturer*. Whether these programs or practices occur in hospitals, churches, civic centers, or elsewhere, they need to create conditions in which parents can successfully explore their initial images of themselves as capable of spiritual and emotional growth through parenthood (9).

Fortunately, this need to support parents in gaining insights into themselves as nurturing persons has prompted a myriad of parent-oriented education programs and practices. "Becoming a Parent" and "Learning about Parenting" classes are now available in virtually every community in the country. Unfortunately, in too many cases the content of these courses is limited to the immediate concerns of birthing, to handling specific mechanical tasks of early parenting, and to the special needs of a given parent (114). Some encouraging signs that birthing and parenting courses offered to parents during pregnancy are changing are the emergence of new topics and the extension of these initial experiences to continuing educational offerings for parents. It appears that the early work of professionals like Gordon (44) and others (24, 34, 70, 129) is now beginning to take hold in the more widespread practices of parent educators and family-support professionals. A few examples of the strategies being used to encourage the development of this nurturing orientation in parents follow:

- Engaging parents, especially fathers, in self-assessments of their supportive attributes as they have developed them over a period of time.

- Involving parents in nurturing situations where they can see the affective side of their development in a direct manner.

- Encouraging parents to plan not only for the physical and work-role changes that come with parenthood but also to ponder the need for their focusing on the nurturing roles.

Even more encouraging is the emerging involvement of teachers and other school personnel in participating in the development, support, and implementation of these experiences (75). While still far too isolated from each other, schools and other family-support programs such as Head Start, WIC, and Preschool Special Service Programs are beginning to collaborate on sponsoring a variety of partnership-promoting activities with parents of infants and toddlers. Begun in 1967, *Parent-Child Centers* have served as parent and family-support resources for parents of infants and toddlers within the Head Start Program (87). Another outgrowth of Head Start were the *Child and Family Resource Programs*. While changing in nature, the focus of these programs has been on strengthening parents in their self-image and skills as growing persons who can continue their growth through parenting. Extensions of the emphases of these programs on parent self-image, healthy family beginnings, and building partnerships between family and community are now evident in *Family Resource Centers* across the nation (106). These programs have taken many different forms: drop-in centers, library programs, counseling and referral clinics, and combinations of center- and home-based services. A distinct feature of many of these emerging programs is their emphasis on involving all parents in relationship-building experiences that prevent occurrence of at-risk family situations (106).

Whether the parent education experiences are offered by schools, hospitals, churches, or community agencies, or in a collaborative mode, the primary goal is to begin with the parent as a person and extend outward toward the roles and relationships that make for healthy family beginnings (1, 37, 113, 115). A signficant part of this learning process should engage parents in forming images of how their new status as parents influences the need for new roles, new resources, new skills—all of which can be approached in a developmental manner (60).

This learning process becomes even more significant in at-risk contexts where parents confront or are enveloped by abusive or degrading situations (1, 43). Parental impotency, often prompted by a person's past or present experiences with abuse, is or should be the focus of efforts to resolve the at-riskness. Powell's review (93) of home-visiting programs includes insights on some projects, such as the Family, Infant and Preschool Program of the Western Carolina Center, that use a multifocused approach to alleviate or resolve conditions that are impeding parenting and family life. These conditions are the risk factors that indeed have been related to children's failure to achieve in school or life and have also been related to many pathological behavior patterns among parents and families (12, 41, 72). They include the six at-risk indicators identified: chemical abuse behaviors, antisocial personal/parental life styles, malnutrition, illiteracy, poor health care, and ineffective home-learning ecologies (91). Most observations note that these indicators are interrelated with factors such as poverty and psychosocial deficits (3, 14, 26, 41, 82).

In such contexts, parent education and family support strategies are focusing on helping parents and families gain control of the forces that are eroding their power, attempting to enable them to regain the sense of self-worth and self-direction essential to having a positive basis for being a parent (128). Home-visiting programs, carried out by trained professionals with assistance from paraprofessionals, combined with intensive intervention efforts (professional counseling, family support actions, and therapy programs) have focused on assisting at-risk parents to resolve issues during the family's formative period (43). Some of the common threads present in many of these efforts are: helping parents to acquire family basics such as housing, food, and clothing; supporting parents in their efforts to acquire necessary life skills such as job training; engaging parents in resolving at-risk behaviors such as illiteracy and socioemotional pathologies in the family; and helping parents to gain the needed information and skills for strengthening their understanding of children and of themselves as persons and parents

(43, 84, 86, 106). Recent research strongly indicates that some or all of these indicators are present across socioeconomic lines (115).

In essence, the initial focus of efforts to promote strong parent-teacher partnerships must be on early parenting behaviors—those behaviors and attributes formed prior to the child's third birthday. The emphases should be on the critical roles parents carry out—nurturing, teaching, and modeling—and on their engagement in acquiring an understanding of themselves as worthy and capable individuals who can enter into healthy marital and family relationships and extend their empowerment through continuing partnerships with a variety of helpers (23, 40, 91, 115). The failure of teachers and other helping professionals to enter into early, formative partnerships with parents and families has been the major missing link in attempts to shape strong, positive connections between families and schools (95). By the time of school entrance, parents as well as teachers have already internalized their images of how relationships should occur and have already applied them in their interactions with children, related community groups, and indeed, in their family relationships (94, 114, 115).

Parents: Having Meaningful Relationships with Children

A natural extension of parental learning about the key roles of nurturance, teaching, and modeling occurs as they form relationships with their children (105). With a sense of self-confidence gained only through their growth, the development of knowledge, skills, and attitudes for relating positively to children becomes a priority for parents. Through the process of maturation, parents gain a realization of their role in supporting, guiding, and teaching children (37, 40). It is important to recognize that in this search for meaningful ways to relate to children, parents want and should have a significant part in determining how they will proceed; in effect, developing a parenting orientation that is sensitive and unique to their identity as it takes shape (93). The tragic scenario of parents experiencing "helpers" who hinder more than they help has distorted parental conceptions of the partnership process (70, 112).

Parents' involvement in shaping their parent education experiences is imperative to having a partnership concept emerge that is truly reflective of a sense of mutuality between them and their helpers (91, 92, 97, 105). This involvement is evident in recent parent education program directions that use various ways to invite input from parents on what should be included in courses, study groups, and other learning modes (15). As Powell (92) and Pence (86) note, the move toward a meaningful parent-professional relationship includes the observance of the integrity of both; neither sees the other as simply a client or as a professional but rather as concerned and capable partners with much to contribute to each other and to children.

One example of this more growth-oriented approach to parent education and family support is the *Family Literacy Project* (21). While the focus of the project is on at-risk parents and children, the strategies used are relevant to programs oriented toward the parent population in general. The project is an attempt to improve education of at-risk families by going beyond the confines of the classroom. It provides early intervention to break the cycle of illiteracy by combining efforts to provide quality early childhood education with strategies to improve the literacy and parenting skills of undereducated adults. In addition to providing parents with information and skills on parenting and child development, the program makes every attempt to relate to the particular needs (as seen by the parents) of the parents and families being served. Through the inclusion of components such as early childhood education, adult education, parenting education, and vocational development, program personnel are able to relate varying parent needs to specific services available (21). One positive feature of the parenting education aspect of the program is that it actively engages parents in experiences where they are both supporting their children in positive ways and doing learning activities with them and skilled caregivers.

An example of how this component is organized and carried out follows:

> Two specific times in the school day were developed to address parenting education needs. During Parent Time (PT) the parents, along with a teacher, design programs of interest to study and discuss. PT is usually scheduled for 45 minutes after lunch while the children are playing outside. PT discussions include such parenting topics as nurturing, disciplining, accessing community resources and parent/child communication. Parents as Teachers Time (PAT) involves the parents and their children in preschool activities that stimulate and reinforce interaction within the family. Parents are encouraged to let the child lead the play period. Parents learn how to teach while playing with their child. (21, p. 34)

Clearly, these early experiences with teachers offer parents and teachers opportunities to be involved in supportive roles where they are helping children and each other develop a literacy orientation toward life. In addition, and very critically, parents are engaged in proactive experiences with children and teachers, developing insights into ways that they can become more engaged in partnership-building activities (21).

Another very promising effort to engage parents in developing healthy relationships with their children and their helping team is the *Parents as Teachers* (PAT) project (129). This program is based on solid research regarding the critical areas of children's early development and learning. Initially the program was piloted in selected school districts in Missouri and guided by the work and insights of Burton L. White (129). The broad goal of providing educational guidance and support for parents of children during the first three years of life was a result of the research and the pilot studies. The project, now offered in schools throughout Missouri, attempts to demonstrate how schools, in partnership with families, can help children achieve the best possible start in school and life. It is available to all parents and centers on the common educational needs of families. Services include information and guidance to parents prior to the birth of the baby; information about what parents should attend to in terms of the child's social, language, and cognitive development; periodic health assessments for the child, especially as related to vision and hearing; a parent resource center at the school site; monthly home visits; and monthly group meetings. The program, guided by local advisory councils, is an excellent example of how teachers and parents can begin their partnership in a positive way prior to the beginning of the formal school years (115).

In establishing the critical roles of nurturing, teaching, and modeling through the guided support of caring early childhood professionals, parents develop skills they will use throughout their relationship-building endeavors: observation, teaming, supporting, learning, doing, responding, and assessing. Beyond the obvious value of closer parent-child relationships that seem inherent in the PAT and similar programs is the value of parents' involvement in articulating what is good for the child, for their personal growth, and for their emerging relationships with helpers such as teachers.

One outcome of our increasingly complex social ecology has been a growing number of at-risk parents—parents who need special support and, in some cases, intensive intervention. These at-risk parenting situations are increasing and cloud the nation's future more than any other social or economic issue (106). Traditional parent education strategies will not suffice to address the complex needs of parents embedded in pathological behavior syndromes such as alcoholism, other drug abuse, or other pathologies (20, 31, 70, 95, 115). Yet there are successful approaches being used to engage these parents in positive experiences with their infants and young children. One very promising effort along these lines is the focus on reaching potentially at-risk parents, before they become parents, through educational efforts in high schools and community settings. These efforts must be directed toward the perceived needs of adolescents and must include a very caring, responsive atmosphere. Delivering knowledge alone to young people will not suffice; a multidimensional approach that combines knowledge with counseling, career support, and critically-emotional support—as is the case in the Johns Hopkins Program—is essential (106).

Resource Mothers is yet another innovative, highly personal program that reaches teen parents before the baby is born (106). With a focus on gaining the trust and involvement of these very young soon-to-be mothers, Resource Mothers provides needed information on prenatal care, parenting, and support resources, and, just as important, offers continuity of help so that the risk factors being confronted can be dealt with effectively. Similar intensive intervention projects, many related to drug abuse and poverty, are realizing the benefits of combining parent learning related to child development to parent learning about themselves as important people who can gain the literacy skills for lifelong success (106).

The solid foundation that is established early in life by parents in their positive relationships with infants, toddlers, and young children is a powerful influence in their gaining the sense of confidence needed for partnership endeavors (40, 41). The work of Ira Gordon (44) in the Florida Parent Education projects was significant in the observation that as parents gained in skills for better relating to and engaging with their children in language, social, and related play activities, they also gained in the self-image skills needed to see themselves as capable of nurturing relationships. This is no simple achievement and should not be taken as a skill that all people develop. Rather, the early relationships of parents with children are the empowering moments that strengthen parental control skills as well as stimulate their growth toward reaching out to others effectively (9, 35, 66).

EARLY PARTNERSHIP EXPERIENCES OF PARENTS

Parents, like all human beings, build a system of relationships that enable them to carry out life's many functions (67). Whether in the workplace, at church, or in a family, people build partnerships in order to negotiate the many dimensions of life that require a team approach (77, 86). There are some valuable insights on how parents develop these partnerships and what they mean to their development as parents as well as to their children's learning and development. The process of "nest-building," which is a combination of various relationships, begins prior to the birth of the child (67). Galinsky (37) notes that parents rehearse various elements of parenting including the relationship-building processes. In this rehearsal, parents "image" themselves as important people in the lives of their child and develop ideas on how they are going to structure their lives to accommodate the new demands of being a parent (37).

This nest-building process typically begins with parents refining their partnerships within a small circle of intimates, typically relatives and close friends. *Indeed, the lack of close intimates may disrupt or impede parents as they attempt to create meaningful partnerships during the early years of family life* (77, 86). Parent involvement in these early partnerships focuses on many of the same issues that they will later experience in contacts with schools and other community groups. While the issues may be somewhat more oriented to basic child and family arrangements, their substance is similar to those issues confronted when the child enters kindergarten. They still require the parent to negotiate relationships with other adults so that the process of growth can occur (66, 77).

A hallmark of this early partnership-building period is in parental attempts to construct a support system (and then refine it as the family develops) that best nurtures the family to respond to the changes of life (115). For example, a new mother may have already made arrangements with a friend or relative to care for the baby while she shops or attends to tasks that require her close attention. She may, in turn, help her "helper" with spring cleaning as a "thank-you" for the help received with the baby. Such help-exchanges are common in this partnership development process (101). Other behaviors such as information-sharing, problem solving, and supportiveness are common to all partnership endeavors. As with any new experience, parents seek out resources that will enable them to fulfill their image of themselves as being good parents. Building viable partnerships is a significant part of imaging oneself as becoming a competent parent (101).

Even in cases where parents may not have access to their close intimates in the physical sense (because of geographical isolation or death), they form psychological relationships that support their efforts at building a support system (37). It is not uncommon, for example, for a young parent to form a new relationship with a person who represents the qualities they valued in a close intimate who is no longer physically accessible. In effect, early partnership-experiences of parents are often connected to their images of what a supportive person should be like (37). The desire for a *mentor* quality in at least a few of one's partners is a healthy indicator that parents have a desirable image of how they want to be as a parent. It is also a signal that they realize the need to have friends who can support their family's growth (77). Indeed, some evidence suggests that when parents have a choice, they seek caregivers who have at least some of the qualities they sought in friendship networks (37).

Two additional features of these early partnership-building experiences are seeking validation and the desire to be productive (86). The challenges of early parenthood create a strong need in parents for validation of their competence or for their potential to become competent. This need is met through strong partnerships with close intimates or through relationships with helping professionals who have the ability to humanize their involvement with the parent (37). In effect, the parent is asking for a vote of confidence in her/his worth as a new and growing parent. Through many discussions, interactions, and nurturing experiences with significant others, parents may resolve this validation issue enough to support their continued growth. Later, parents will repeat this process as they interact with their children's caregivers and teachers, in effect asking for support for their identity and not just for their child's. Growing parents also want to contribute to their helpers and to the community. They seek, through their partnerships, a sense of mutuality that they too are helpers, not just receivers of help (40). As Powell (91, 92) so aptly notes, early parent education groups may serve more of a support function in this sense than purely for information or skill-based purposes.

An extension of this partnership-building process occurs with the birth of the child and continues with the many transactions parents complete during the child's first three years of life. It is a time that parents must integrate their highly intimate circle of helpers with the more formal system of helpers—physicians, nurses, social workers. This is critical for parents as they attempt to accommodate and integrate the community into their nest-building. What is often overlooked by professionals is that parents are very vulnerable at this point and that they seek both help and support not just for the infant but also for themselves (37, 77, 86). *Highly negative and/or sterile experiences with hospitals, community agencies, and even with schools at this early, formative stage can influence parents to avoid later partnerships, or place them in a mental framework of being an adversary rather than an advocate and supporter of the helping professions* (115).

It is these early relationships with the formal systems that are supposed to support in parents images of a lasting nature that are constructed with regard to how partnerships actually occur (86). And, as the helping professions have institutionalized their practices of helping, history shows that the needs of parents have often been homogenized, thus reducing the intimacy of some very significant experiences in their lives such as the birthing process and the "entering child care or school process" (68). Fortunately, sensitive professionals, often moved to action by parent advocates, have begun to see that birthing and child care are indeed partnership experiences not to be mechanized and treated as purely medical or educational events. It is hoped that the sterile, lonely delivery room of the 1950s is being replaced by a more intimate, trusting, and honest environment where family is present to support the parent-team in beginning their journey toward growth.

In positive, supportive partnerships where parents and physicians and caregivers are in a nurturing alliance, the key elements of partnership-building can take shape in parents and be refined and extended in their helpers (97, 101, 105). This calls for a learning approach on the part of professionals, fully sensitive to the dramatic growth taking place in parents. This is an opportune time to help and encourage parents to "take control" (within reasoned limits) of the birth, nurturance, and sustenance of their child (23, 37, 105). For it is in this arena that the basic elements of the partnership-building process occur: realizing the personal and professional strengths of each other; coming to know each other as "in partnership" and "in trust" with regard to both family and community-building; joining in mutually beneficial actions that promote the health and well-being of all who are a part of this relationship; solving problems through a verbal and nonverbal dialogue that establishes respect for each other; and extending the benefits of this new relationship to later

65

family growth as well as to helping others in the community become a part of this covenant (9). Olds et al. (84), in describing an especially designed parent education program for at-risk parents of infants, best depict what kinds of partnerships should be pursued:

> Parent education was the first major activity. A basic premise of the program was that a sense of caring and a strong alliance between nurses and parents were necessary ingredients for successful outcomes. In the context of trust and respect, parents would be more likely to accept the advice and support of home visitors. The nurses tried to establish this emotional tone by listening to parents' concerns, showing respect for family members, and sharing some of their own experiences as parents. As part of this educational process, the home visitors strove to strengthen the mothers feelings of adequacy and self-confidence, give them more control, and reduce their guilt. (pp. 34-35)

It is in this kind of context that the seeds of positive and meaningful partnerships can be nurtured in parents. Olds's conception of the partnership process as grounded in a caring, responsive relationship system is indeed the direction helping professions should pursue (84). The *Minnesota Early Childhood Family Education program* approach is a fine example of an attempt to carry out the ingredients of a viable system for having meaningful parent-helper relationships (28). This statewide program, which is actually a structure that allows for a diversity of local programs, is based on the premise that all parents have strengths and that the period from birth to six years of age is just as critical for parents as it is for young children. Further, the program is based on the strong belief that decision making on services and activities needs to be centered within the context of each community, allowing for, and indeed encouraging, the intimate involvement of parents and citizens in building systems that they perceive as meeting their needs (28). This active-partnership approach comes through in Engstrom's (28) description of what parents seem to gain from being a part of a support group:

> In group discussions, parents discover strengths they never realized they had. Their self-esteem seems to soar when several parents react positively to their way of handling a specific situation. (p. 14)

This is indicative of a partnership that recognizes that trusting relationships can only take shape when parents have a strong influence on both the content and the process of the nest-building that will serve the family through many growth adventures (86).

Building on the idea that parents' early experiences in establishing partnerships with other intimates and helping professionals is absolutely critical, Family Resource Centers are emerging in many communities (106). These centers focus on the family as a center of potential strength rather than as a deficit-oriented paradigm. In line with the philosophy of nurturing strength, these centers are engaging parents in shaping the mission and structure of the programs in which they participate. The "parent as leader" construct has credence in this approach as parents are seen as the center of action whether it be in counseling, parent education, child-care referral, health, or other basic services (115). Further, these programs are attempting to educate citizens and professionals in a new mode of thinking and acting with regard to the needs of families, especially families with young children. Encouraging pediatricians, nurses, social workers, churches, schools, and businesses to "think family" is a significant part of the mission of Family Resource Centers (88).

Through the realization of successful early partnerships with their network of intimates and skilled helpers, parents can construct a positive family system that supports their growth in the key roles of nurturing, teaching, and modeling; strengthens their faith in the potential of the community as a place for them and their children to grow in healthy ways; increases their self-confidence as capable persons and parents; enables them to acquire the needed attitudes and skills for having continuing and meaningful partnerships with their helpers; and engages them in contributive experiences where they extend their parenting to advocate for the needs of others (22, 40, 44, 66, 80, 92, 96, 105, 109, 114).

DEGRADING PARTNERSHIPS: TRAGIC ENCOUNTERS OF AT-RISK PARENTS

The ever-increasing number of at-risk parents (parents who confront various problems that erode their integrity to function) endangers the entire society (106). In many cases these situations are the result of multiple factors including constitutional and ecological events and influences. Some of the significant factors and influences that have been identified include poverty, illiteracy, chemical dependence, antisocial personality orientation, homelessness, and combinations of these factors. The outcome of these influences is often seen in a lack of parental control skills, a poor self-image, extreme developmental delays related to carrying out basic parenting roles, and a highly disorganized social network of relationships (14, 35, 43). In particular, these influences appear to create a life system that is often characterized as follows:

- Parents lack a basic knowledge of their role as parents and often feel no identity with regard to their self-worth (12).

- Parents have little understanding of how children develop and learn, and often lack even the basic information on how to care for children (27).

- Parents are often engaged in confronting multiple pathologies (whether self-inflicted or brought on by environmental factors) such as poverty, drug abuse, illiteracy, and other such impediments (14).

68

- Parents are often extremely pessimistic, lacking any faith that they or their family can improve with planning and effort (41).

- Parents are often lacking in employment, job skills, have difficulty dealing with change, and may give evidence of mental disorganization (26).

- Parents lack mentors, intimate friendships, and often have few social support resources (86).

- Parents lack financial resources to sustain adequate food, housing, and health care for self and family (27).

- Parents often lack the developmental skills for setting a direction for self and family (14).

- Parents may have a personal history that has influenced their "risk" condition in degrading ways (82).

These attributes of *risk* often appear in multiples that are naturally interrelated (one influencing the other with an eventual umbrella of risks permeating the parent's life) and thus require more than the usual attention. Just as infants at risk require major intervention for survival, so *at-risk parents* require intensive and continuing support and education (106). Additionally, these attributes too often emerge in vital parts of our populace: young, single parents; poor, illiterate teens; unemployed, minority parents; chemically dependent parents, and parents who themselves have or are experiencing severe abuse/neglect (27). Yet, these attributes also appear, with ever-increasing numbers, in all segments of the population where they may not be as observable until they reach crisis proportions (9).

Lacking a sound psychosocial and spiritual foundation, at-risk parents have not only been short-circuited in their own development but often experience human relationships within a negative context. For example, crack mothers often are on the receiving end of degrading partnerships from the only source of comfort they might have access to—helping professionals (106). Likewise, homeless parents are often chastised for their lack of motivation and/or their lack of life-coping skills. Unfortunately, the deficit approach to helping at-risk parents prevails in reality, if not in theory (70, 105). The deficit model, which aims to correct a specific weakness (often out of context with related issues), approaches relationships from a set of assumptions that are certain to create conditions that degrade and further weaken parents. For example, parents confronting at-risk situations are often given help in addressing an issue that is inherent in a dysfunctional social system and that is likely to lead to high recidivism in the particular issue being treated. Parent educators, as an example, often bemoan the lack of observable changes in at-risk parents who have received intensive educational intervention without realizing that the problem is beyond simply providing parents with educational tools; the social structure must be changed. Consider the homeless mother who knows how to access health care for herself and her child but is told that until she has a permanent address she does not qualify for the care (3). Also consider the father who has successfully completed drug-rehabilitation counseling but is turned away from job after job because of his past record (3).

Until recently the deficit paradigm was (and too often still is) followed in hospitals, social work, and even in pastoral care and schools. In effect, the needs of at-risk parents have often been homogenized into a negative pattern that places the parent in a degrading and often misconstrued context. This erroneous and damaging view of at-risk parents is vividly portrayed by Atkinson in her presentation on the powerless position many homeless parents are placed in by the system:

> Laura could not find shelter for her and her three-year-old in Charleston (South Carolina) and thus "hiked" to Columbia. Here she at least found a place at night in the Salvation Army. But each morning they must leave by 6 a.m. (shelter rules). She has tried to get care for her child and ended up at our

center for homeless children. In trying to get her more permanent shelter we ran into the "wall"; the get-in-line syndrome. In job hunting, she found rejection the norm as her dress and lack of a "home" became hidden but powerful forces of degradation in the minds of her interviewers. Laura not only needs "supports" but a more responsive system; indeed, a society where knowledge and skills can work. (3, p. 3)

Even where the system seems to be more viable, the mental images people have of those who are at-risk are predominantly negative, degrading, and cynical. The pediatric nurse who short-changes the teen-mother "cause it won't do any good anyway"; the preschool teacher who turns a child away because "he's headed for trouble for sure"; and yes—even the pastor who evades the at-risk parent "cause I've done what I can do" are present in the risk relationships of far too many parents.

Empathetic-ecological approaches are being piloted in attempts to reshape our partnerships with at-risk parents and children during the earliest periods of childhood (86). For example, hospital-sponsored parent support programs are exploring the mentoring/sharing approach by matching a first-time, at-risk parent with a supportive parent-mentor from the community. In this way they hope to personalize the new parent's first experiences in parenting (84, 103). Through this experience many single, at-risk parents find the friend they need for support, information, and for the closeness so vital to good beginnings (84). Mentors often receive training on the importance of their supporting the person's growth in positive ways and of working with them as a partner in this learning process of becoming a parent. This use of capable, sensitive, and caring nonprofessionals in nurturing and guiding roles helps—at least in some respects—to meet an extended-family need in a new way (106).

An important part of this mentoring process is the "partnership learning" that mentor and mentoree experience.

Parents confronting at-risk situations and/or involved in behavior patterns that place them and their infant in fragile contexts have opportunities to acquire skills and behaviors both for proactive problem solving and for relating to others in helping and supportive ways (106). In far too many cases at-risk parents have lacked appropriate role models for acquiring the attitudes and skills for working effectively in partnership contexts (115).

Programs such as *The Nurturing Center,* a child-abuse prevention center in Columbia, South Carolina, are placing their primary emphasis on positive ways to support at-risk parents in the development of skills that they can use in gaining control over their lives through various means: parent education, comprehensive health care, job training placement, employment counseling, therapy, and related services (82). The intent in these programs is to strengthen parental integrity by engaging parents in a partnership by which they can eventually acquire the skills for shaping a healthy environment for the family (105).

Given the focus of supporting at-risk parents in developing more mastery of their self-image and their environment, collaborative, intensive methods of parent education and family support are achieving more success than the traditional approaches (93). This is especially the case with parents who are lacking in any self-direction or self-confidence. Similar to the nurturing center concept is the Family Resource Center. While some family resource centers are primarily oriented to walk-in parents, many are now focusing on collaborative arrangements with other helping professionals to address the critical needs of at-risk parents during the family's earliest years of development (106).

TEACHER PERCEPTIONS OF EARLY PARTNERSHIPS

While teacher-parent partnerships are historically embedded in the early childhood education construct, the context of current social and professional systems have discouraged the full development of this orientation (115). In the early part of this century, and through many of the programs piloted during the 1930s to the present time, parent coops, parent-teacher study teams, parent involvement in the classroom, and other such strategies were commonplace in early learning and development programs (114). However, with the dramatic changes in families, in the workplace, and throughout our communities, the partnership construct suffered from both new societal values on a mechanistic approach to education and from the shift of both parent and teacher priorities toward simpler, more isolated interpretations of their respective roles with children and each other (51). In a sense, the deficit-oriented paradigm, which has permeated many of the early intervention programs, encouraged more limited teacher perspectives regarding parent involvement.

For example, in some of the early intervention-focused programs, the emphasis in concept and practice was on the child's deficits (105). The child-only focus (a client-centered one-dimensional approach) was neat and simple; treat the child's deficit and progress should occur. Indeed, some of these early efforts did document child progress, albeit only for the short term (105). In far too many cases the mechanistic approach was of limited value, with children often regressing soon after the "treatment" ended. Further, insightful observers were noting the decrease in parents' engagement with children as experts took over responsibilities once shared by parent and teacher. Gordon (44) and others (2, 23, 40, 86, 105, 114) challenged this limited construct of early learning and influenced the beginning of a broader more empathetic-ecological perspective. This broader perspective placed children's learning and development within the ecology of the family and the larger systems of the community (41).

As with any new concept, the adoption of the empathetic-ecological perspective has been gradual, at least as far as gaining any large-scale acceptance within educational institutions. The major reason for resistance to this broader, parent-oriented philosophy is that it requires a restructuring of how we carry out early childhood programs as well as of how we conduct business in schools, communities, and in the workplace (19, 22, 40, 86, 126). In the family-centered philosophy, parents are seen as the key leaders in creating opportunity through carrying out significant parenting roles (nurturing, teaching, and modeling) and in their critical partnership roles of supporting, learning, doing, and decision making (105, 115).

Ironically, this more parent-sensitive construct emerged at a time when both parents and teachers had become comfortable with the simplicity of the more traditional models of functioning. The rigid demarcation of the parent/professional roles was, and to some degree still is, a comfortable position for avoiding any conflicts or any genuine partnership building. It has permeated most of the helping professions and to a large degree has impeded the growth of the very people who are supposed to be about the business of supporting each other in becoming growing and positive individuals (105).

Lightfoot (70) highlights the damage that evolved from this simplistic perspective: the dehumanization of the parent; the artificial and impermeable wall placed between family and school; the exploitation of both parent and helper; and the seeding of tensions that certainly emerge in contexts that encourage distrust. Perhaps Suransky's (112) ethnography on the erosion of childhood is more an indictment of the myopic philosophy prevalent in too many early childhood contexts than it is an attack on the helpers themselves (22).

Researchers such as Schaefer (105), Epstein (30, 31), and Swick (114, 115) have presented data that suggests that limited teacher perspectives regarding parental roles in children's lives has influenced partnership building in negative ways; and yet with appropriate training and support for teachers and parents, these conditions are alterable. For example, Schaefer (105) found that teachers perceived the parent-involvement process to be more one of clarifying the role of the teacher and delineating to parents some basic ways they (the parents) could help than a process of mutuality. These same teachers did not rank the "parent as educator" or the "parent as decision maker" roles as highly signficant to the child's education or to the parent-teacher partnership. Gordon (44) found a similar situation in attempting to pilot various parent education models. He designed teacher and paraprofessional training experiences to counter this limited vision of the parent as simply a receiver of help. He noted several success stories where teachers and paraprofessionals not only broadened their views of parents but also initiated more activities with parents. In particular, Gordon (44) noted that empathetic parent views regarding teacher roles in family-school partnerships were more likely to emerge in relationships where teachers were exemplary listeners.

Swick (117) also found that parent-involvement training that was oriented toward broadening teachers' views of parents as related to the partnership process was influential in increasing teacher initiatives in the desired direction. In particular, he noted that direct teacher-parent relationship assignments (teachers visited the home of a parent and carried out an informal dialogue on the child and family's needs and strengths) were most effective in challenging teachers' stereotypes of families. Further, it has been found that teacher training, correlated with other signifi-cant support variables, was a positive influence on teacher initiatives related to supporting mutuality in the teacher-parent relationship (122).

Desired teacher perceptions and behaviors related to having partnerships with parents during the early childhood years include many dimensions: an understanding of their roles as related to partnerships with parents; a realization of empathetic-ecological perspectives in relating to children and families; the recognition and use of parents' skills and talents in the development of programs; a sensitivity to the personal and cultural strengths of parents and families; an orientation in the designs and strategies appropriate for use in developing strong and positive partnerships with parents; and a clear sense of the mutuality that permeates successful relationships (113). Even in exemplary parent-oriented early childhood programs these teacher behaviors are never fully realized. There are strong ties to the client-deficit and/or rigidly defined teacher-parent role paradigm (105). There are, however, some encouraging practices that are emerging that reflect a more empathetic-ecological orientation toward the desired partnership process.

EARLY PARTNERSHIP STRATEGIES FOR TEACHERS

The following strategies have been found to be effective:

- Involvement of parents and teachers in discussions about parent education issues such as child development and the management of children's learning environments (124).

- Involvement of parents, teachers, and health professionals in collaborative assessment activities related to children's health and development (124).

- Formation of teacher-parent support groups that focus on strengthening the ties between the child's primary educators (44).

- Utilization of home visiting as a means of providing parents and teachers a time for exploring their common concerns, sharing information on child development and learning, and laying a foundation for having positive relationships (93).

- Formation of parent-parent support groups within early childhood settings to promote both educational and social goals that parents define as critical to their family's well-being (93).

76

- Initiation of one-on-one, teacher-parent dialogue orientation times where, before the child begins school, teachers and parents have an opportunity to probe each others' ideas and feelings related to the learning and development process (23).

The promotion of even more intensive teacher-parent partnership strategies that reflect the empathetic-ecological approach such as the in-classroom involvement of parents in reading/tutorial/sharing experiences and the engagement of parents in participatory management of the classroom system are needed (22). Yet both limited parent/professional visions regarding their relationship and the inhibiting nature of current school system structures have impeded the full exploration of these strategies. As Swick and McKnight (120) noted in their study, teachers tended to be more fully responsive to having shared partnerships with parents when time, resources, philosophy, training, and system elements were supportive of it.

The emergence of a more empathetic-ecological perspective related to teacher-parent partnerships is evident in the work of programs such as *Avance* (128), *Parents as Teachers* (129), *FOCUS* (115), and other similar parent-oriented early childhood projects. While these programs may confront major challenges with regard to carrying out a truly mutuality-based approach, they can serve as case studies for what should and must emerge throughout all early childhood programs. The need for exploring new structures, strategies, and perspectives related to engaging parents and teachers in early, supportive, and nurturing partnerships is critical to long-term educational and social improvements (2). In addition, the positive actions of many classroom teachers in piloting innovative teacher-parent partnership strategies in their classrooms, described in Chapter 5, will serve not only as a means of enriching their learning environment but also as a testing ground for other professionals to observe.

Chapter 5

A FRAMEWORK AND STRATEGIES FOR TEACHER-PARENT PARTNERSHIPS

Once teachers and parents have developed a foundation for having meaningful relationships, an empathetic-ecological framework that is accompanied by the use of effective strategies can promote strong teacher-parent partnerships. Integral to this framework are several philosophical points.

1. Teachers and parents must have a sense of respect for each other's integrity, for their abilities to grow and develop in positive ways as individuals and within their respective roles (40).

2. Teachers must be sensitive to the possible limitations of their orientation toward parents as it may have evolved within a mechanistic, deficit, oriented system (34, 70).

3. Parents must be cognizant of the dynamic role of teachers as it relates to planning and carrying out good quality early learning programs (1).

4. Teachers and parents must recognize and respond to the serious limitations in the ways that schools are currently structured (114).

5. Parents and teachers must articulate and actualize a commitment to carrying out the needed planning, dialogue, and responsive involvement essential to their partnership (113).

6. Teachers and parents must continually strive to become "children's advocates" through the significant roles of nurturing, teaching, and modeling (114, 115).

Some indicators of this philosophical foundation follow (113, p. 3):

Parents and teachers work toward common goals in a mutually supportive manner.

Teachers involve parents in curriculum-related decision making and improvement efforts.

Parents and teachers communicate on problems and concerns in an open and honest fashion.

Teachers and parents engage in shared-learning experiences.

Parents and teachers engage in "helping" roles that strengthen both the classroom and the home learning ecologies.

Clearly, these partnership indicators are based on another vital element of the empathetic-ecological framework: teacher-parent partnerships are or should be developmental and growth-oriented processes.

Inherent in the developmental view of parent-teacher relationships is the premise that parents and teachers can, through intentional efforts, build a relationship that is continuously growing, expanding, and refining itself. This view, then, does not accept the notion that certain parents [or teachers] are unable to develop as full partners in home-school relations. Rather, this perspective sees each parent [and each teacher] as an individual capable of growth, developing their skills in an interactive manner. (114, p. 119)

Further, this construct holds that parents and teachers can experience a series of developmental levels by which they can strengthen their individual identity and, in turn, enable each to be a more effective partner with the other (114). It is within this developmental context that Rich (96) noted that all parents and children have the substance of learning within their families; it is

79

simply the task of sensitive teacher-parent partnerships to probe the potential through various home-learning strategies. Sensitive teachers (as well as parents) recognize the presence of growth in parents and in themselves, thus realizing that partnerships are dynamic and not static or mechanistic.

THE DEVELOPMENTAL NATURE
OF TEACHER-PARENT PARTNERSHIPS

While there is no rigid sequence to the development of teacher-parent partnerships, there is a set of dynamics that represent the manner in which they take shape. This process has usually started before parents and teachers actually have contact with each other. Both parents and teachers usually begin the partnership process by reflecting and imaging the roles they should carry out (37, 105). Depending on their prior relationships with other helpers and their roles with children, teachers and parents differ widely on how they conceptualize their part of the partnership process. Hopefully, both have had some learning experiences in this regard such as teacher training courses or parent education experiences. One clear advantage to the early involvement of parents and teachers in relationship-building processes is that they have more experiences to use in constructing positive images of this vital alliance (114, 116). This process of imaging one's roles (nurturing, teaching, modeling) will continue over the span of time in which partnerships are pursued. The continuing involvement of parents and teachers in this reflective process is vital to their growth as persons who are engaged in a dynamic relationship (113, 114, 115).

The initial contacts that parents and teachers have with each other (opening of school, preschool orientation) are typically devoted to feeling out each other with regard to expectations, roles, styles of interaction and related issues that influence their partnership (114). This period is critical because it is when teachers and parents begin to articulate their ideas on what and how their partnership should work. It is a time when their mutual roles of learning, supporting, doing, and decision making begin to take on some meaning. Many schools have recognized the essential part this period plays in the child's education and have set aside orientation and discussion times for parents and teachers to use in establishing a solid beginning (114). It is in these early contacts that teachers can establish the basis for an empathetic approach, assuring parents of their vital role in their children's education and offering them meaningful ways of engaging in the process (6, 22). This is also a natural time for parent-teacher dialogue on the common mission they have as well as on the unique and common roles each can contribute to the partnership (105).

As teachers and parents establish a foundation for their relationship they usually begin to explore some of the ways that they can assist each other in achieving their mission; this may include setting objectives related to specific nurturing, teaching, and modeling roles as well as to the mutual roles of supporting, learning, doing, and decision making. Naturally, these objectives will reflect the varying stages of development in which parents and teachers are functioning and reflect the various needs they see as important. For example, parents who are new to the school may center much of their energy on clarifying their roles, probing on how they can get involved, and learning about the program in which their children are enrolled. This is a time when teachers can invite parents to become a significant part of their children's learning both at school and at home (80). Experienced parents and teachers are likely to extend their perspectives to include more sophisticated partnership activities such as shared decision making and advocacy strategies.

Emerging from teacher and parent exchanges regarding ways that they can support children and each other is the development of some form of systematic involvement plan. This may be accomplished in several ways: regular conferences, periodic meetings, planned parent-involvement activities, parent-teacher learning sessions, and through various other means. Each partnership, depending upon the school's arrangements and the unique attributes of the parents and teachers involved, will organize a system of relationships that are supportive of their needs (114). An empathetic approach to this process will emphasize the sensitive and responsive involvement of teachers and parents in joint endeavors.

As parents and teachers develop strength in their relationships, they arrive at a point where two attributes emerge: a more "focused" relationship (the partnership acquires a sense of distinct purpose along with an organized problem-solving perspective); and a sense of being a part of a larger mission, that of being advocates for other children, parents, and teachers. Energy is now focused on particular concerns such as supporting the child's development of a special talent or meeting a specific parent or teacher need. Rich (96, 97) notes that parents and teachers have found their most meaningful efforts to be those that center on curriculum, behavior, and home-learning strategies that are within the reach of all parents. Parent and teacher advocacy efforts, while initially very specific to their concerns, typically expand to include the concerns that influence all children (51). Examples of this outreach aspect of the partnership include participating in joint efforts on school improvement; promoting public awareness of critical family-school needs; and supporting local initiatives that respond to the need for quality early childhood programs (51, 115).

A natural and essential part of the sequence of growth in partnerships is the arrival of parents and teachers at a point of mutuality, where interests and commitments are not only well understood but also pursued with a sense of long-term involvement. A sense of solidification and refinement is evident in the partnership and mutual concern prevails. Each respects the other's uniqueness and developmental orientation and works toward helping the other (and self) grow in the process. A visible indicator of this aspect of the parent-teacher partnership is the involvement of both partners in strategies that support their concerns as well as the concerns that affect the total community (114).

Naturally, the dynamics of actual relationships between teachers and parents occur in a more spontaneous manner than this scheme suggests, including the influences of parent and teacher contexts, education, personal motivation, and cultural and social perspectives. Yet, the sequence portrayed provides a system by which a framework for meaningful teacher-parent partnerships can be actualized.

A FRAMEWORK FOR TEACHER-PARENT PARTNERSHIPS

Building upon the understanding that teacher-parent partnerships are developmental in nature and that an empathetic-ecological approach is most conducive to achieving strong partnerships, a framework for organizing, supporting, and carrying out the process is essential to having successful ventures (114). The following are elements that need to be reviewed in terms of their influence on this framework: (a) teacher and parent contexts, (b) teacher and parent role understandings, and (c) teacher and parent understandings of the nature and dynamics of parent involvement (113, 116). While these influential factors have been examined in previous sections, they must be integrated into the planning and implementation framework. Otherwise, the steps and procedures used to create meaningful partnership activities can be impeded by a lack of understanding by teachers and parents of their roles, contexts, and commitments (39). Further, a sensitivity to each others' needs, situations, and talents is a requisite to having a solid basis for carrying out desired plans. Each parent-involvement program should reflect the unique situations, needs, talents, resources, and commitments of the teachers and parents involved. Indeed, the real value of having a systematic framework for planning teacher-parent partnerships is that the process should reveal both the most likely focus of a partnership for the parents and teachers involved and provide the means by which this process can become a reality. Figure 6 provides a picture of the basic elements of an early childhood teacher-parent partnership planning framework.

Figure 6
Teacher-Parent Partnership
Planning Framework

TEACHER BASES   PARENT BASES
Perspectives   Perspectives
Context   Context
Role Understanding   Role Understanding

PLANNING PROCESS

Needs Assessment
Goals/Objectives
Setting Priorities
Selecting Strategies
Organizing Resources
Designing Implementation
Continual Assessment

IMPLEMENTATION STRATEGIES

Dialogue as Foundation
Conferencing
Home Visiting
Parent/Teacher Learning
Involvement via Technology
Home-Learning Strategies
In-Classroom Parent Involvement
Group Meetings/Activities
Other

EVALUATION ACTIVITIES

Feedback
Refinement

Needs assessment provides the arena for promoting partnership activities that are both meaningful and supportive of long-term possibilities. It should engage teachers and parents in ventures where their individual and common perspectives, roles, and situations are articulated in terms of desired experiences and outcomes (128). This process might occur in various ways: parent orientation meetings, conferences, study teams, home visits, parent education programs, or a combination of these modes. Through continuing discussion, teacher and parent perspectives can begin to emerge as a partial basis for needs identification. Figure 7 is an example of perspective statements developed by one teacher-parent team.

Figure 7

Teacher Perspective	Parent Perspective
Provide child/parent with a stimulating and supportive learning environment.	Support our children in being successful learners.
Communicate with parents on my clear expectations regarding the children's behavior and learning habits.	Communicate with our children about appropriate behaviors and attitudes for successful learning.
Provide the family with a context in the classroom that is inviting, orderly, and responsive.	Support the teacher by providing our children with a positive learning environment at home.

Teacher-Parent Perspectives

Engage in joint planning and doing activities that enrich both the classroom and the home learning environment.

Offer each other support to better carry out our teaching and nurturing roles.

Participate in continuing communication activities that positively and yet realistically strengthen teacher and parent positions for having successful relationships.

Through "perspective taking," parents and teachers can shape an agenda of needs areas that reflect their individual and common concerns. Areas typically but not always included in such assessments are learning needs unique to individual teacher and parent perceptions; support roles and activities that each can help with; program needs (early childhood curriculum, facilities, resources); communication needs; planning and decision-making needs; and implementation issues (15). Teachers have found various means, in addition to personal contacts, to gain parent input: questionnaires, study groups, conferences, group meetings, and especially through the natural feedback provided by parents within the context of the program (114).

The needs-assessment construct also provides teachers and other school leaders with an excellent opportunity to examine their orientation to the parent involvement process. It is critical for teachers to carry out periodic reviews of their partnership philosophy as well as of their knowledge and skill basis for being effective partners. Further, this process should include a thorough assessment of the resources needed to carry out an effective program (32, 55, 56).

Data generated through truly responsive and engaging needs assessment can provide the basis for usable program objectives. An initial step is to cluster identified needs into categories that represent a common purpose. For example, the *Minnesota Early Learning and Development* program (MELD) found that parents had a common need for basic child development, parenting, and family living information (28). Rich (96, 97), in her work at the *Home and School Institute*, found that parents of young school children had a common interest in knowing what was expected by the teacher, what behavior guidelines were expected of the children, and when and how they were to communicate with the teacher. This cluster of needs could easily be organized into a parent-teacher communication category. Likewise, the teacher may have specific needs that can be related to an involvement/decision-making cluster. For example, needs may exist for parent volunteers to help with special events, parent representation on program-planning teams, and parent-teacher dialogue on special issues related to the learning program (30, 71).

Once needs clusters have been organized, parent-teacher planning should focus on setting priorities. With limited resources, prioritizing can support the goal of having a partnership vision that includes both immediate and long-range goals. This process is more than a formal system of rank-ordering needs; it requires the sensitive response of teachers to the expressed and observed needs of everyone involved in the teaching-learning process. For example, informal parent interactions provide valuable feedback on their perceptions of priorities that may not emerge within formal settings (92). In some cases parents may not feel comfortable listing certain support needs that may appear too sensitive for open discussion. Swick shares an example of one parent-teacher group's list of priorities in Figure 8 (114, p. 124).

Figure 8
Parent-Teacher Program Needs

High Priority

Establish better teacher/parent communication.
Involve the community more in classroom projects.
Develop an extended-day enrichment program.
Organize a child-development program for 3- and 4-year olds.

Long-Range Priorities

Form a summer enrichment program for families.
Organize a classroom-based teacher/parent planning team.
Develop a parent volunteer program.

Partnership objectives take on meaning as they emerge through this needs-setting process. An important consideration is the process that is established for parents and teachers to use in creating a real sense of mutuality. The learning process should be seen not only as a partnership but also it should be actively pursued in this manner. In addition, stated objectives should provide the framework for teachers and parents to pursue activities they both support. The communication and feedback process also allows for continuing refinements in plans as well as a means for clarifying the roles and functions of everyone involved (114).

The active involvement of teachers and parents in carrying out desired objectives requires a thorough review and selection of useful strategies. Finding a match between needs and strategies is a process that each team of parents and teachers will carry out in relationship to their context. For example, while some programs have found home visits to be an ideal home-learning strategy, others have been more successful with school-based parenting-education programs. Swick (121) explored the use of multiple strategies with parents in four different settings and confirmed that each partnership approach selected strategies that best suited their unique needs. Some of the examples Swick (121) noted in this regard are briefly summarized:

One classroom found tremendous success with conferences; parents not only responded positively to this strategy but extended their involvement by requesting follow-up contacts.

Another classroom (in another district) had more success with home visits and informal teacher-parent contacts than with other strategies. The teacher believed that because of the rural setting (families lived considerable distance from the school), parents relied on home visits and the telephone to maintain involvement with their children's learning.

In-classroom involvement proved very successful in a class-room that was located in a small, intimate kindergarten-primary school. Parents lived close to the school and were, in a sense, very close friends of the teacher. They were highly supportive of her program and often modified work schedules to be able to participate in classroom activities, field trips, and special events.

It was noted that offering parents multiple opportunities to be involved in their children's education increased the potential for strengthening teacher-parent partnerships (121). Such an approach broadened the teacher's vision of parents as true partners and as able to achieve many tasks that they had not previously credited parents with being willing to undertake. There is yet another insight worth noting: as parents became involved in one mode of participation, their overall interest in other dimensions of the partnership increased.

Implementation of teacher-parent partnership efforts can be supported through consideration of various issues both in advance of and throughout the program's activities. Questions such as the following are helpful in this process:

- Are program activities reflective of the needs that emerged through formal and informal teacher-parent planning opportunities (97)?

- Are the planned activities well organized, with partic-ular people assigned to handle needed tasks for making them successful (80)?

- Have the program activities been planned at times convenient for parental participation and have notices of the plans been sent to parents (122)?

- Are the resources needed for carrying out various activities available and organized for use (114)?

Assessment and refinement of partnership activities is essential to the growth that should emerge as a distinguishing feature of parent-teacher relationships. Feedback, renewal of goals and leadership structures, and extension of parent-teacher efforts are vital to successful programs (128). Feedback can be obtained through regular assessments of program activities by the participants, through annual evaluation surveys, and through various other means. Informal narrative reports by parents have proved quite useful in bringing about program improvements. One of the more direct and powerful assessment tools is dialogue between parents and teachers (31, 96).

The ultimate goal of any partnership is to reach a stage of growth where the individuals involved have both a sense of emotional involvement and the cognitive tools for pursuing a continual strengthening of their relationship. One tool for reviewing how teacher-parent partnership frameworks are working is shown in Figure 9 (114, p. 131).

Figure 9
A Teacher-Parent Partnership Framework Checklist

—Teacher-parent involvement in assessing priority needs has been conducted.

—Identified needs are being used to plan partnership endeavors.

—Program activities reflect a coherent and logical relationship to the needs established.

—Strategies selected to carry out various objectives reflect the desires and needs of those involved.

—Specific program activities are well organized with specific individuals assigned to monitor their success.

—Needed resources and facilities for carrying out activities have been organized and prepared in advance.

—Adequate notice of planned events has been prepared and sent to parents.

—A process for refining and improving the partnership has been developed and used.

SUCCESSFUL PROGRAM EXAMPLES

Successful early childhood teacher-parent partnerships are characterized by their focus on enhancing the quality of early learning and development (92). It is in the mission and the process that exemplary partnerships are born, not in the packaging—nor even in the housing of such efforts. Programs that focused on the very early years such as Parents as Teachers and Family Resource Centers as well as many other programs that serve parents of preschool-age children have exemplary attributes such as the learning and support activities they generate. In effect, success is in the emerging involvement of parents and teachers as they seek to strengthen home and school learning opportunities for their children and themselves. The following are some examples of kindergarten-primary grade program efforts that deserve attention.

A Rural Partnership for School Success

This program was developed as a pilot project (partially funded by the U.S. Office of Education) with the very specific mission of enhancing the school success of at-risk kindergarten and first-grade children through strengthening teacher-parent partnerships. Ninety children and their parents and teachers (thirty children in each of three schools) participated in the project. The central focus of this program was to provide a comprehensive learning program in which teachers, parents, and home-school-leaders would acquire a variety of skills to strengthen their individual and collaborative efforts in supporting children's learning in school and at home. The design engaged teachers and home-school-workers (paraprofessionals who received special training) in efforts to involve parents of children who were academically at-risk in training and activities that would strengthen their position as teachers of their children at home and in classroom contexts (121).

Each home-school-worker—one in each school—devoted her/his efforts to carrying out strategies that engaged parents and teachers in individual and collaborative learning and involvement roles with each other and with the children. A curriculum focus centered on four key concept learning areas: language, mathematics, social responsibility, and expressive attributes. Computer literacy activities were integrated into all of the curriculum efforts. Typically, one home-school-worker (HSW) served three teachers and thirty parents/children in their school. HSWs usually spent about half of their week in activities related to the classroom and the other half in efforts directed toward parent involvement. Functioning as "bridge-builders," the HSWs organized many of the training and involvement activities to bring teachers and parents into contact with each other.

Major partnership-building strategies used in the project were home visits, parent-training programs (in which teachers were involved and often served as resource leaders), conferences (involving teachers, parents, and HSWs in various combinations), home-learning activities (each classroom had a home learning center), in-classroom involvement of parents, a computer home-loan program, take-home videotaped parenting programs, and informal involvement activities. A sampling of the activities carried out through the use of these strategies include:

Parent training on topics such as "How Children Learn Math," "How Children Learn Feelings," and "Parents, Teachers, and Children: Learning About Computers Together."

Home-learning activities included specific learning games parents could use with their children as well as books and other materials they could share with their children.

In-classroom involvement activities included the involvement of parents in working with a child or a small group of children on key concept learning areas (often on the computer) or in assisting the teacher in carrying out a group activity (121).

Throughout the project an effort was made to bring parents into close contact with their children and their children's teacher(s) in learning situations that directly related to the children's success. For example, when the children were learning to read a book like *Kelly Bear Feelings,* parent activities were related to this focus. Parent-training sessions revolved around the book and the processes involved in children's learning how to express and relate to their feelings. A copy of the book was provided for each family and parents were encouraged to discuss the book and to share with their children stories of feelings they had when they were children. Some parents came into the classroom and read to their children; others helped the children make mobiles of feelings for display throughout the school. A similar process was used with parents who could participate only through home visits. This design of "matching" classroom learning emphases and home-learning activities proved to be highly successful; it was a way that all parents could engage in learning activities that had a direct influence on what their children were learning at that time. Indeed, a highlight of the year was the shared-learning experiences of children and parents as they acquired computer usage skills in various training and involvement modes (121).

Data generated through an assessment of this pilot project provide some key insights on designing early childhood teacher-parent partnership efforts. One of these insights relates to the nature and structure of parent-involvement activities during the early childhood years—a time when most parents are highly interested in their children's development and learning. By organizing involvement activities that draw parents into the

94

center of children's learning, the potential for creating a supportive orientation in the parent-child relationship is greatly increased. Further, the intimate involvement of parents in school- and home-learning strategies that directly influence the children's school performance certainly strengthens their position as teachers of children and increases their linkage to their child's teacher at school (121).

Another insight worth noting was the observation that a diversity of parent and teacher partnership-building strategies did indeed increase the levels of parent involvement in children's education (121). The inherent advantages in offering parents and teachers multiple opportunities to engage in shared efforts are worth the extra work and resources put into this critical process (121). While this pilot project had additional resources to achieve an increased emphasis on parent involvement, most schools could achieve many parent involvement strategies with some restructuring of professional/paraprofessional roles and with the reorganization of classroom instruction. Some advantages realized were increased participation of at-risk parents in all involvement categories; improvements in teacher and parent perspectives toward each other's roles in the education of their children; and a noticeable increment in teacher-parent contacts (121).

Additional insights that emerged from the Teacher-Parent Partnership project and that have been supported by the work of others (29, 30, 32, 53, 58, 69, 98) include: parental participation rates in school- or classroom-based activities increases when support resources such as child care and transportation are available; teacher initiatives regarding partnership-building increase with training and school support resources; diversity of parent involvement strategies is especially influential in stimulating parents, who traditionally remain isolated from the teacher, to get involved; the presence of fully trained paraprofessionals in the role of home-school-workers strengthened and extended the amount and quality of parent-teacher interactions possible; and the involvement of parents in program support roles increased their perceptions of themselves as capable people (121).

Learning Goes Home

The "learning goes home" construct evolved from the work at the Home and School Institute (HSI) by Dorothy Rich and others (96, 97). The foundation of this partnership approach is the "parent as teacher" or "parent as tutor" idea. Inherent in this design is the recognition that parent-teacher partnerships are best initiated through activities that emanate from children's learning as it occurs within the classroom. Rich states:

> The involvement of parents in the education of their own children means building a program as it should be built, from the bottom up, rather than from the top down. It creates a foundation of support and commitment for other kinds of involvement efforts. It may also obviate the need for many other kinds of public relations efforts as families begin to understand what is really involved in the education of their children. (96, p. 57)

Further, this approach is based on assumptions that all families are in a position to become meaningfully engaged in school- and home-learning efforts:

- All children have experiences that are meaningful to them; some children's experiences are simply different.
- Home environments, no matter how poor, are places of care and concern for children.
- All parents have the abilities, when properly supported, to help their child succeed in school.
- Family potential can be readily activated into practical support for children and schools.
- Teachers, in search of promoting parent involvement, should start with family strengths, not with their deficits.
- All teachers can initiate some form of positive home learning through positive relationships with parents.

96

The learning-goes-home approach is best realized when it is initiated during the family's formative experiences with school. It enables parents and children to see and actualize a supportive learning role of what occurs in the school through complementary learning efforts at home. It also encourages families to see education as a shared responsibility (96).

A key strategy used in this approach is the *Home Learning Recipe.* "Recipes" are specific, practical, no-cost activities for learning at home. During the early childhood years these recipes focus on experiences parents and children can carry out within their natural contexts of living: cooking activities, sharing of books and magazines, story-telling, family sharing times, and many other activities. The goal of these experiences is to build healthy family relationships and a foundation for skills for school success (96). Various school and community groups have used the HSI design or adapted it to their situation with success.

Based upon the success of the HSI approach, Rich (98) further refined the model with the development of *MegaSkills.* In a sense, these are skills that are needed before children can fully engage in the acquisition of school-based skills. As Rich states:

> It is generally agreed that children need certain basic skills (usually called the three R's) in order to succeed in school. But, for children to learn these basic skills at school, they need to learn another important set of basics at home. I call these "MegaSkills." This is the curriculum that is taught at home. It's reinforced in the classroom, but, mostly it has to be taught by the family (97, p. 90)

These MegaSkills include the behaviors, attitudes, and constructs that children need in order to be full partners in the learning process. Rich's (98) MegaSkills include: Confidence, Motivation, Effort, Responsibility, Initiative, Perseverance, Caring, Teamwork, Competition, Common Sense, and Problem Solving. Through a design that is built around appropriate activities for varying developmental and age ranges, one can build an early childhood MegaSkills curriculum for the home.

Research on the learning goes home design has indicated a high level of success (97, 98). A synthesis of the findings indicate that family participation rates (per school engaged in using the design) typically range from 60 to 90 percent; teachers have consistently reported that parents who participate in HSI-supported programs have become more involved in multiple aspects of their children's education; participating parents report various personal indicators that reflect a strengthening of their self-image; school administrators see the program as highly valuable; and parents and teachers have observed children's school performance to improve (97, 98).

Family Math

Utilizing an especially designed curriculum of math learning experiences, many early childhood teachers have found impressive results with the "family math" program. The program is designed to involve parents in their children's education; to introduce families to key mathematical principles; to develop students' critical and logical thinking skills; and to connect mathematics to everyday life. The central philosophy of family math is to help children and their parents see mathematics as an intrinsically enjoyable area of learning (107). While the program has a specified design, many teachers have adapted key parts of the program for use in their classroom-based parent-involvement activities.

The design involves two major components: a training program for teachers (and interested parents) that equips them with the skills to carry out a series of family math workshops with the parents and children they teach; and workshops (typically six to eight sessions are held) that engage parents and children in actively learning key principles of math. The math principles that are the primary focus include: measurement, arithmetic, estimation, geometry, probability and statistics, logical thinking patterns and functions, and algebra.

Family math training workshops (usually including 12 hours of instruction) typically run for two days, with instruction based on 30–40 minutes modules. The modules focus on specific topics such as logical thinking, fractions, calculators, and arithmetic. The atmosphere is informal and involves participants in hands-on math activities. Parents and teachers who participate in the training together report a shared-learning experience in which they gain many ideas not only on how to improve math learning but also on how to function as supporters of each other's teaching and learning efforts (107).

The family math workshops or classes take on many forms and yet have a central purpose: to engage family members in enjoyable learning activities related to the key principles of math. Teachers use a wide variety of materials (beans, paper clips, rice, straws, computers, calculators) in carrying out the course structure as set by the *Family Math Book*. While the book provides the overall structure for the sessions, teachers adapt it to the needs and interests of their families. Shields and David describe part of a session they attended:

> Next we move on to measurement. We take strings and cut them to match our partner's height (each adult is paired with a child). We then estimate the amount of times the strings will wrap around our wrist, then our head, then our midriff. I glance around the room. Families, who just a half an hour earlier looked as if they were about to receive an incomprehensible lecture, are standing on tables, wrapping strings about one another, pinching each other's fat, laughing—and being introduced to concepts of estimation, measurement, and spatial reasoning. (107, p. 30)

The emphasis in class sessions is on involving family in enjoyable math learning. Some teachers have found that by serving a light meal, providing transportation, and offering the workshops on a repeat basis, they have achieved close to 100 percent participation. By keeping the sessions active and limited to 60–90 minutes, family participation is greatly increased.

In addition to bringing families together to enjoy learning as a joint activity, family math has had some other important influences: bringing parents and teachers into regular contact with each other, providing teachers with a broader understanding of the children and parents they teach, increasing parent involvement in children's education in general, improving children's performance in math, and providing a beginning for having other family-school involvement activities. Indeed, many teachers have used family math as one part of their overall partnership efforts with families (106).

The three teacher-parent partnership projects reviewed here have some common ground in relation to fostering positive partnerships: they focused on something specific to the child's learning; each used a diversity of resources and strategies in involving parents; the focus of each program was on something positive teachers and parents could pursue; they involved parents in the planning and assessment process; each addressed the unique concerns of the families they were serving; and they fostered attitudes and activities that encouraged long-term partnerships. Beyond these and other formal program examples are a variety of partnership strategies and activities that teachers and parents can use to strengthen their positions as leaders in children's education.

PARTNERSHIP STRATEGIES

The changing nature of family life over the past thirty years and the growing acceptance of an empathetic-ecological perspective on the critical role parents play in their children's education have prompted teachers to explore the use of a variety of partnership-building strategies. This is especially significant in early childhood education where parent involvement has been related to the healthy development of the child (15, 40). With no particular sequence, a number of teacher-parent partnership strategies, resources, and activities are reviewed here. These strategies are most effective when they are developed and carried out within a framework such as the one presented earlier. Further, these strategies need to be related closely to the context of the teacher, the parents, and the children engaged in the partnership.

Home Visits

Home visits have proved especially useful for working with parents of infants and toddlers and with families who have special needs that may preclude their participation in school- or center-based activities (13, 22, 52, 93). This strategy has many distinct advantages: it encourages parent and teacher to see the home as a learning environment; it allows for demonstration of home-learning strategies in the setting where they are to be used; it sensitizes the teacher to the realities of each parent's situation; and it offers parents a chance to share their family's history. Of course there are cautionary issues such as making sure parents are comfortable with this strategy and that the "visitor" is well trained (93). In addition to the many educational activities that can be delivered, this opportunity for close contact between teacher and parents is invaluable for building trust and empathy. Teachers of children who are in child development, kindergarten, and primary grade programs have found home visits to be supportive of their mission to integrate classroom learning habits and attitudes into the parent-child relationship (114, 122).

Objectives for home-visit programs range from the emphasis on instruction to a more support services orientation. Powell (93) notes that most programs have multiple goals and use the home visit as one element in their attempt to involve parents.

For example, in the Parents as Teachers program, home visits are used to carry out instruction with new parents on basic child care and development strategies and also as a means of providing parents with supportive services (129). A real strength of the home visit is that it provides a personal setting where teachers and parents can explore many different ideas on children's learning as well as on their own growth.

Home-visit programs are usually organized around themes that reflect particular emphases. Depending upon the nature of the project or program, home visits may be scheduled on a weekly, monthly, or less consistent basis. Visits may range from 30 minutes to an hour. Most successful programs rely on a continuing system of visits in order to establish trust with the parents and to maintain a program that has a continuing influence on the family. One such program (121) held monthly visits (each visit lasting about 45 minutes), with the substance of each visit focusing on a key learning area that was being carried out in the classroom.

Early childhood home visits are often used to link parents more closely with their child's teacher. Home visitors, for example, might use the visit to arrange for the parent to participate in classroom activities, in school-based parenting programs, or to engage parents on school-improvement councils. Programs that use home visits on a continuing basis have found an increase in parent involvement in other school activities (93, 122).

Several strategies have proved effective in the planning and use of home visits. A well-organized plan is a key to success. Establishing a clear purpose, organizing the visiting activities, responding to parent needs, and involving parents in the visits are important organizational steps. Advance preparation of parents for the home visit through telephone calls and written notes also proves helpful. Being responsive to the unique situation of each family is a potential strength of the visiting process (31, 92).

Instruction is a primary function of most home-visit

programs. Activities included in home visits usually are based on key learning skills, are short and basic tasks that parents can do with their children, and are related to ways that parents can improve the family's relationships. Some examples of activities include sharing books with children, using objects in the home environment as learning resources, introducing new vocabulary through language experiences, sharing stories with children, carrying out planned learning games, doing family activities together, and supporting/encouraging children in home and school involvement (80).

Training Programs and Study Groups

Parent training and education programs have been a successful part of most early childhood education programs. Training emphases have included specific parenting skills; particular activities for supporting children with developmental and/or special needs; specific child development skills such as language; and, in some cases, directed home-learning activities. Educational emphases usually have revolved around topics familiarizing parents with the school or center's programs, information on appropriate expectations and experiences for children, home-learning strategies, ideas for strengthening parent-child relations, ideas for helping parents respond to homework, orienting parents to new curricula, and so forth. Study groups, while not as widely used as in the past, offer parents and teachers a system for continual learning and sharing (15). Indeed, the more open-ended and parent-guided these groups are, the better the possibilities are for meaningful dialogue between parents and teachers (20).

One particular use of parent training in schools that has proved quite successful is parent-oriented education. Examples of themes used in schools or classroom-based parent education are "How Children Acquire Language," "Developing Self-Esteem in

Young Children," "Health and Safety at Home and School," and many related themes. In addition, teachers have found group sessions to be useful in providing parents with information on new curricula, orientation to classroom policies and practices, and on issues of common interest to parents. Some programs have used videotapes of sessions as a means of reaching as many parents as possible (97, 122).

One of the most popular parent education sessions has been on the topic of discipline. The focus is usually on ways in which parents can apply positive discipline practices in the family's relationships. The content is based on child development, what to expect from children at different stages of development. Programs use role-playing, films, discussion, and other techniques to involve parents in activities in which they can practice supportive ways of improving their relationships with children (15).

Conferences

Both short, informal miniconferences and the more formal conferences offer multiple partnership opportunities such as sharing information, getting feedback from each other other on mutual concerns, offering each other support, sharing and resolving concerns, planning school-home-learning strategies, and carrying out various child-support strategies. In addition to planned conferences, regular informal contacts provide opportunities for many supportive activities (92, 114). The value of teacher-parent conferencing can never be taken for granted; it is a process where support, problem solving, sharing, listening, and meaningful planning can lead to a very productive school-family relationship.

Scheduling and planning conferences related to parent needs is crucial to their success. Providing an inviting, supportive, and confidential setting is important. Strategies that make for successful conferences include (79, 80):

- Planning the preconference thoroughly
- Creating a comfortable setting
- Encouraging parent questions
- Being accepting and responsive
- Allowing for active parent participation
- Using meaningful follow-up activities.

Newsletters and Notes

Classroom-developed newsletters (especially those where children and parents have input) are excellent for keeping everyone informed about what is happening in the classroom, the projects being carried out or planned, and for the sharing of family-oriented material such as new books or special family television programs, and so on. This is a way of reaching all parents. Newsletters that emerge from the classroom are usually of high interest to parents, especially when their children have had a major part in producing them. Notes home on children's progress, children's special achievements, parent reminders of planned activities, and requests for help have also proved useful. "Newsletter Calendars" that include monthly information of interest to parents and children are valuable. These calendars may include menu information, forthcoming classroom activities, special events, parent-teacher meetings, and other important information. Technology has made this strategy efficient and creative and has also increased parent awareness of what is happening each month at school (6, 22).

Most parents enjoy and use newsletters, especially those that have items of concern to them. Effective newsletters involve parents in the design and content, include items about what the children are accomplishing, are attractive, and are easily posted in the home. The content of newsletters varies and might include helpful hints, classroom events, calendar of school activities, ideas on parent involvement, highlights of children's achievements, needs of the classroom, and many other items.

Lending Libraries/Learning Centers

This is another early childhood strategy that can potentially involve all of the parents. Depending upon available space and resources, lending libraries and resource centers vary in their scope, size, and mission. Typically, lending libraries contain materials, games, books, tapes, and related resources that children and parents can borrow for home use. For example, parent-oriented materials (depending upon the purpose of the library) are often focused on themes of interest to parents (often parents are surveyed to determine these needs). Learning centers usually have a broader mission. Vartuli and Rogers (125) describe such a center that is housed in a library system. It is organized with a room unto itself and is open for about four hours a day, with monthly themes providing the focus. Activities center around things and resources all parents have access to such as kitchen utensils or available library resources. Classroom teachers have used this concept with many modifications, often identifying it as a "home-learning center." These centers often become a launching pad for many other teacher-parent activities such as study groups, support groups, or adult education projects (125). An inviting feature of these library/resource centers is their accessibility to parents and children. This is a strategy in which busy parents can participate, based on their needs and schedules (114).

Welcoming Parent Strategies

Early childhood teachers value their early contacts with parents. Ball (4) provides several excellent ideas in this regard: always greet families with warmth; provide children and parents with a clear idea of how your program works (brochures, videotapes, and newsletters are some tools for this purpose); hold opening-of-school orientation programs; develop a "common questions that parents ask folder"; post specific times for parents and children to give you feedback (one teacher calls these "teacher listens" times); and encourage parents to be a part of the classroom. Additional welcoming activities include light meal socials, planned phone calls to each family, and "praise a family" greeting cards (4, 20, 33, 55, 56). Warm, supportive relationships with parents establish the foundation for long-term partnerships. Introducing yourself as a person (sending personal notes to children before school opens) is as important as introducing yourself as the teacher (4). Opening meetings with parents should be personal, warm, and inviting, offering them opportunities to get to know you as a person who cares about children.

A Communication Potpourri

Given the dynamic and complex lives of parents and teachers, many kinds of communication are needed. Beyond the more traditional ways of conferencing and written communications, there are several informal and yet very effective strategies: telephoning parents about reminders of activities or brief updates on the child's progress; daily recorded messages on homework tasks and/or key ideas that were covered in class; once-a-week "homework hot-line" reviews; and technology-based exchanges (fax, modem access, interactive home-school closed-circuit programs) (5, 6, 120). Here are some more partnership communication strategies: send home weekly student-work folders, weekly "notes home" on work covered that week, "Parent-Grams" that go out once a month and review key ideas covered in class; set up a parent bulletin board near the most parent-traveled areas of the classroom or school; call parents for monthly feedback; hold small-group parent dialogue times; hold morning coffees with parents; have parents come to lunch on a scheduled basis; help parents develop a "parent support newsletter" for sharing concerns and support with other parents; and develop a "Parents Only" News Sheet (33, 75, 78). The list of communication strategies is indeed endless. Consider: setting up a "homework notebook for parents," holding a "family fun dinner" once a month (sponsored by parents and children), holding enjoyable parent-teacher learning times, and sponsoring a parent-help program (6, 15, 20, 33). Parent-teacher partnerships that have frequent and meaningful communications are usually positive and growing (114). Many schools are finding that training programs in which teachers and parents learn about communication skills and strategies that they can use to strengthen their partnership are effective in increasing the positive involvement of parents in school programs (121). Further, staff development programs on sensitizing teachers to the cultural and social backgrounds of their parents is also proving to be valuable in gaining more effective parent involvement (34).

Parents as Helpers

In spite of dramatic changes in, and increased demands on parents, they are finding ways to support children and teachers in enriching and strengthening the classroom learning environment. Helping strategies range from parents doing short-term tasks such as reading to children to highly organized parent volunteer projects. The modeling influence of parents and teachers working together in the classroom is, by itself, justification enough for the effort that goes into organizing it (114). Indeed, this strategy offers a chance for teachers and parents to plan a program of in-classroom involvement that is well organized and relevant to the particular needs of the children and the program (114). For elaborate programs, the following elements need close attention: specific emphases to be addressed, clarification of roles "helpers" are to carry out, provisions for needed orientation and training, delineation of scheduling and related management issues, and periodic team communication sessions (113, 114). The following are examples of activities carried out by classroom helpers:

- Tutoring individual children
- Shared-reading activities with small groups of children
- Interacting with children in learning centers or tasks
- Assisting with the preparation of classroom learning materials
- Sharing a special talent or skill with the children
- Helping out during high-stress times of the day.

Technology and Home Learning

Many teachers and schools, with community support, are experimenting with the interactive uses of technology as a parent-child involvement mode (25, p. 7a). Four such pilot projects offer some very interesting ideas that might be modified to meet specific teacher and classroom situations.

1. "Homework Hot Line," run by Instructional Television Center in Broward County, Florida, is produced by the public schools for Broward County's 160,000 children. Help is given by classroom teachers on a variety of subjects.

2. In Chicago, "Homework Helpers" airs three times a week for children in grades 1-4. Teachers present and discuss problems similar to the ones presented in class.

3. In Sacramento, California, two programs focus on homework: "Words Work" and "Math Help-Line" (one hour each). Both programs offer in-depth help on English and math once a week.

4. "Dial a Teacher" (Fairfax, Virginia) has answered math questions for viewers for five years.

The programs are most effective when parents are involved with their children during the viewing. In other cases, individual teachers are setting up hot lines where parents and children can call for help.

More Strategies on Homework

In some dimension, homework provides parents with an avenue to become an involved parent (95, 98). The goal is not for parents to do the homework but rather to support their child in becoming a successful home learner. This may involve parents in making sure that children have a time and place for doing homework and, most important, that they act supportive in this process. Parents should also take note that the more they model and encourage good and enjoyable learning habits such as daily reading, the more likely it is that their children will acquire these same good attitudes and habits (61, 71). Teachers are finding that nicely presented idea sheets on enjoyable learning at home can encourage parents in this direction. On the more formal aspects of homework, some teachers are assigning short learning activities for parents and children to do together. Others are setting up after-school help sessions. In addition, taped-phone messages for parents on daily assignments have proved successful. Dial-A-Teacher, Hot Lines, Homework Help Centers, and Computer Home Loan Programs have all proved to be successful in bringing parents and children closer together in sharing the homework process, and in developing more enjoyable home learning habits (25, 33, 113).

Informal Links to Parents

The busy worlds of parenting and teaching require many informal linkages where communication and active support can occur. Some ways to achieve this include weekly or monthly student work samples sent home; sending "quick notes" on children's progress or work; sending "positive notes" on the child's achievements; setting up a parent room or corner just for parents; asking parents to respond to surveys or needs-assessment questionnaires; offering parents short educational programs on new curriculum material (videotaped back-ups are helpful for parents who are unable to attend); and setting up a variety of "home loan" parent involvement activities. These informal strategies enable teachers to reach a broader audience of parents and often lead to parent involvement in more formal activities (96, 97).

Promoting Multicultural Learning

Teachers and parents can be models of cultural and ethnic sharing for children. Many activities can be used to develop this effort; for example, you can sponsor International Night where food, clothing, and customs are shared; you can organize "parent resource teams," where parents can share something about their heritage with the children and other parents; you can involve the children and their parents in doing "family trees" and then create a hallway of our heritage (or display the family histories in the community); and you can bring parents together to learn about the importance of modeling positive multicultural attitudes and practices for their children (16, 34, 59). Another easy access strategy for involving parents is to make available to them print and video materials on the lives of people from different cultures. Most important, you can model culturally sensitive behaviors for parents and children by having bilingual materials available where appropriate, and recognizing holidays and special events of all of the different cultural and ethnic groups in society in appropriate and positive ways (34).

Parents and teachers have a major responsibility to promote multicultural education during these formative years. A quality parent-involvement program needs to address the many dimensions of cultural diversity in positive ways (34). Ask:

- Are we good role models for children to use as they form their attitudes and behaviors toward culturally different people?

- Do we support children in their search for how people in different cultures live?

- Are we actively involved in promoting positive attitudes and actions among the different people in our school and community?

Opportunities for Learning

Parents of young children want to learn about parenting, child development, and strategies that they can use to support these processes. Some schools, such as Dann Byck Elementary School in Louisville, Kentucky (76), are engaging parents in partnerships through learning opportunities that are offered at the very start of the family's life. Cradle School (a school within a school) is a place where parents can learn more about parenting while their children are benefiting from early learning opportunities (76). The parent-learning experiences are based on parent needs as expressed in open forums. Topics for learning and sharing range from "Caring for Infants and Toddlers" to "What Life Is Like for 4's." Innovative teachers in primary-grade classrooms are continuing this process with sessions focusing on "Positive Involvement with Your Child" and "Family Enjoyment," samples of the many topics covered. Capitalizing on community resources, some schools are collaborating with public libraries, churches, and other agencies to create a diversity of parent learning and sharing opportunities (22, 33, 56, 114). The most effective of these programs are those where parents are in a leadership role in shaping the themes for discussion and study and where teachers are participants with the parents in a shared manner (109, 114).

Parents, Children, and Teachers: A Shared Learning Experience

There are multiple topics and themes that lend themselves to shared learning. Learning about computers is one such topic that teachers are finding of special interest to children and parents. Swick (120) describes one program that combined teacher training, child involvement in the classroom, and parent education in a focus on computer literacy. Parents were involved with teachers in sessions on how the computer works and ways that children and parents can use computers appropriately for both home and school learning. These were "hands-on" sessions in which parents, teachers, and children wrote stories on the computer, used art software to create designs, solved math problems together, and carried out many other activities. These sessions were then supplemented with parent-child opportunities to further their skills in individual activities in the "Parent Computer Room." As parents and children became comfortable and skilled in using and caring for the computer, a "home-loan" program was established. In a related project, it was found that the hands-on computer learning involvement of parents, children, and teachers in group settings promoted many spontaneous extensions of teacher-parent contacts (121). Perhaps partnership activities that are highly attractive to parents hold the key to their achieving more extensive involvement in general.

Encouraging Parent Involvement in Decision Making

The security and effectiveness of teacher-parent partnerships require collaborative structures for making decisions. Several avenues are available for promoting parent participation in decision-making roles. The natural responsiveness of teachers to the expressed interests of parents as they occur in individual contacts, informal discussions, and in group meetings is most effective. This is, in a very real sense, a way of informally engaging many parents in a subtle yet powerful means of choice making (92). It is through these spontaneous decision-making experiences that other, more sophisticated strategies can take on meaning. Additional ways of promoting parent participation in this process that require minimal organization are surveys that ask for parent input, daily interaction with parents, observing parent discussions at school events, taking note of parent concerns during regularly scheduled conferences, and conducting telephone surveys of parents on issues related to program changes (20).

Classroom advisory councils, study groups, curriculum assessment projects, problem-solving sessions, and schoolwide improvement councils are some formal strategies used for encouraging a shared decision-making environment. In carrying out these strategies it is helpful to provide parents with guidelines on how the process works, their roles in making it work, and with an orientation to the specifics of the functioning of the system. These collaboration strategies not only have strengthened the classroom learning effort but also have enabled many parents and teachers to develop their leadership skills. Some examples of projects and achievements that have emerged from these partnership efforts include: well-organized parent volunteer projects, effective classroom and school improvement plans, family-centered learning/sharing activities, parent coop-operated extended-day enrichment programs, parent-teacher support groups, and advocacy teams who pursue community, state, and national improvements related to child and family issues (20, 32, 51, 62, 109).

Parents add a new dimension to classrooms and schools when they become involved in the decisions that shape their children's education. For example, in one school a parent resource team emerged from the work of a teacher-parent study team. This resource team was comprised of parents who were willing to share their talents related to the different curriculum themes in the classroom. In another school, the parent advisory council played a major role in restoring funding for field trips in the early childhood program. The following list includes some additional examples of parents' influence in improving schools (109):

- Improvements in the working conditions of teachers
- Support in decreasing class sizes
- Improvements in teacher-parent relationships
- Increases in school attendance
- Improvements in facilities
- Additions of learning materials and resources.

Involvement in Leadership/Advocacy

Emerging from proactive partnerships are many opportunities for parents and teachers to extend and expand their involvement in leadership and advocacy dimensions that reach beyond the classroom. Many schools and communities have reaped the benefits of leaders who acquired their early foundation through involvement in classroom support and mentoring roles. Leadership roles include guiding schoolwide partnerships, initiating stronger community involvement, serving on school boards, involvement in state-level advisory capacities, and many related dimensions (119). Advocacy opportunities and outcomes include: shaping community policies that are supportive of families and schools; challenging harmful conditions that threaten the quality of life for children and adults; educating citizens on the need for quality schools; promoting school-business partnerships; assessing statewide structures as they relate to supporting effective parent-teacher relationships; and encouraging groups to pursue school support strategies at the national level (114).

PARTNERSHIPS: A SYNTHESIS

Some basic rethinking of parent and teacher roles can lead to a system in which meaningful partnership efforts and strategies can be actualized (31). The basis of this restructuring is the recognition that parents and teachers have mutually complementary roles that include both distinct and common elements. Their partnerships, if they are to be meaningful, must be based on a realization of these roles in theory and in practice (114).

As explored earlier, parental roles include the distinct functions of nurturing, guiding, supporting, and modeling for and with their children the habits, attitudes, behaviors, and skills that promote healthy development and learning. In pursuit of actualizing these roles, parents need to engage in continual learning and in collaborative relationships within and beyond the family to support their efforts. In their learning and growth pursuits, parents should seek (and teachers and other helpers should provide) information and resources that strengthen their position to be their children's teachers, and partners with their children's teachers. This effort might include participating in both formal and informal educational and support activities that increase their abilities to nurture and guide their children as well as to more effectively form partnerships with the family's helpers (15, 114).

Likewise, teachers should reconstitute their view of teaching to be inclusive of learning and mutually supportive relationships with parents (30, 31). In this effort there is a need to see their roles of nurturing, guiding, supporting, and modeling as extending to their relationships with parents and the entire family. Reaching out to parents through "Right from the Start" strategies such as sponsoring parent/family learning and support

116

centers and promoting community programs that enhance the formative years of the family's life are symbolic of the desired orientation (2, 21, 29, 92, 105, 115, 124). Further support of this parent/family-centered approach should occur through the continuing involvement of teachers in training and related learning experiences that strengthen their understanding and skills for actualizing proactive partnerships with parents and children during the early childhood years (2, 92, 114).

Together, parents and teachers need to conceive of their partnership as growth-oriented experiences in which they seek to nurture each other toward becoming full partners in their support of children's learning and development (114). In this empathetic approach, teachers and parents must begin their journey with high regard for each other, their children, and the partnership they are seeking to develop. This calls for seeing each other as capable people, for listening to each other (and our innerselves) in responsive and supportive ways, and for nurturing each other toward the full realization of our talents.

The various strategies described in this chapter offer multiple opportunities for teachers and parents to seek out ways to help each other become both learners and advocates on behalf of children and themselves. Yet these strategies can never achieve this mission if parents and teachers lack a framework that nurtures their desired partnership. For parents to expect teachers to care for their children without the needed supports and alliances is irresponsible. Likewise, for teachers to see their teaching role as limited to the children in their classroom is foolish. Only as teachers and parents develop a vision of themselves as highly important and positive partners in children's lives can these strategies carry meaning.

Chapter 6

EVALUATION AND OTHER PARTNERSHIP ISSUES

Teacher-parent partnerships are in constant need of renewal. Without sources of feedback, partnerships often become static, unresponsive, and rigid (109). Unfortunately, assessment of various aspects of partnerships typically is neglected or at best given little attention, which may be because this process is often viewed as only an outcome-guided effort. Yet the evaluation process, especially as it occurs within an empathetic-ecological approach, is essential to every element of the teacher-parent relationship. Interrelated with the need for continuing evaluation are several issues that influence teacher-parent partnerships: articulating the meaning of partnerships, handling role conflicts, dealing with teacher-parent confrontations, maintaining high regard for all who are involved, responding to cultural differences effectively, and relating in meaningful ways to the needs of at-risk parents.

EVALUATION AS FEEDBACK FOR GROWTH

The terms evaluation and assessment imply that one is taking stock of a situation or process. It is this taking stock that should be an integral part of every partnership. Indeed, assessment and evaluation should be the first tools used in the development of teacher-parent partnership efforts. In the development of partnership efforts, early childhood educators need to ask *how and why* their partnership programs took shape (30, 44, 80). What needs are at the foundation of the partnership? Who was involved in determining the needs, the goals and objectives, the strategies? In too many cases these

118

decisions involve parents (and sometimes teachers) in only a cursory manner. There are many examples of where programs have failed because of a lack of parental and/or teacher input in the development process (16, 29, 39, 95). The content of a program may not relate at all to the perceived needs of parents. Or, the delivery system by which parents are to participate may not match their work or family schedules or their interests. In a similar mismatch, the content may be meaningful but not of priority to parents who are engaged in resolving their own developmental needs (38, 93, 109, 114, 128).

There are many ways to assure that everyone who is to participate in the partnership effort is represented in the initial assessment: direct involvement of parents and teachers, engaging paraprofessionals who are also parents (or who relate to parents in their neighborhoods), holding informal discussions with parents (and teachers), and observing the needs of parents and children who attend the school (113, 114). In a sense, this needs-determination process never ends as it occurs in both formal and informal ways over the life of programs (128).

Evaluation and assessment must also attend to the primary claims of the partnership as they emerge within the dynamics of parent, teacher, and child interactions (128). For example, early childhood parent-oriented education designs typically have two sets of claims: one set deals with the more obvious and desired outcomes such as increasing parent understanding of child development or improving parental attitudes toward their children; a second set of claims, which is more subtly defined by the participants within the ongoing structure of the program, deals with issues such as helping each other increase their levels of family support or sharing with each other child-care concerns and resources (30, 38, 40). While not as measurable, these subtle claims deserve very special attention as they often serve as a floor of security and well-being for the more formalized claims. For example, it has been noted that paraprofessional home visitors who were very close to the families

119

they visited spent more time being responsive to these subtle identity needs than did lead teachers who were more concerned with parent education outcomes as defined in their mission (121). Lightfoot (70) noted a similiar process at work when teachers and parents conference regarding the child's status, progress, or needs. In far too many cases we opt for sticking with the observable dimensions of our agenda and fail to be responsive to the subtle but critical parents' agenda. Yet both aspects of our partnerships with parents are essential to having a developing relationship.

When integrated into our thinking, both formal and informal claims provide our early childhood teacher-parent partnerships with dimensions of strength that offer a direction for our working and growing together (38, 44, 56, 114). In collaborating in the process of forming claims, we need to be cognizant of more than the knowledge dimension and the child-outcome dimension. As Powell (92) notes, a balance of attention with regard to the partners' involvement and proposed benefits in family-school efforts is desired. This is especially important during the early childhood years when most parents are themselves in the midst of major developmental shifts (37).

Given the authenticity and utility of partnership claims, teachers and parents need to consider various indicators that will help them achieve these claims: What leadership resources do they have or need to become effective not in simply attaining goals but rather in developing and growing through their collaborations? What kinds of activities do they see as meaningful and doable? How do they hope to support each other and their children in pursuing their desired outcomes? How can they cooperatively shape and refine their partnerships as they explore working together? While these question/indicators may seem cumbersome, they establish the substance of partnerships in the long-term (114).

The elements of sound teacher-parent partnership assessment efforts often not only support the growth of partnerships during the early years, but also provide the partners with tools to strengthen their own identity and development (37). This is not to be overlooked because strong partnerships can evolve only from individuals who themselves are secure and growing. For example, the major elements of the parent-teacher partnership evaluation process (see Chapter 5) can energize the individuals as well as their collaborations. Acquiring feedback on how programs worked, how parents responded to home visits, and a myriad of other activities, not only feeds the growth of the partnership but also provides possible new ways of living for the participants (128).

THE MEANING OF PARTNERSHIPS

Many problems that arise within the school-family relationship can be traced to misconceptions of what meaningful partnerships are about (2, 20, 34). Program evaluations have consistently found the following attributes to be indicative of parent-teacher partnerships that are misconceived: either teachers or parents attempt to dominate the decision-making process; inadequate arrangements for acquiring a balance of input from the participants; over-reliance on a few participants to handle the leadership roles; isolation of certain parents or teachers from the involvement process; reliance by some participants on using pressure to achieve their goals; and a variety of other misconstrued strategies and indicators (2, 39, 51, 114).

The early childhood years provide an excellent opportunity to address the issue of what meaningful partnerships should be about. It is during this period that teachers and other helpers can initiate educational, support, and collaboration activities that engender in parents an active, growing sense of their critical roles as family leaders. Likewise, through meaningful contacts with parents, teachers can establish themselves as family educators (38, 51). Through continuous planning and dialogue, parents have opportunities to see the professional teacher's role as guide, helper, and supporter of the family's mission. This interactive process of parent-teacher collaboration is filled with many growth experiences; each supports the other with regard to acquiring an understanding of their roles as well as the strength to carry out these roles (59, 76, 83, 114). In the evolution of this relationship-building process, parents and teachers can explore many of the essentials of true partnerships such as the following:

- The involvement of each in the decision making process (109).

- The development of high regard for each other's integrity and roles as advocates and guides for children (22, 32, 38, 97).

- The creation of empathetic and supportive attitudes toward working with each other (114).

- The realization that each has unique and yet common roles to contribute to the processes of development and learning (105).

- The essentiality of their responsiveness to each other's perceived needs and interests (2).

- The focus of their efforts on nurturing each other toward a sense of mutuality that engenders in them a valuing of the well-being of all children and families (22, 40, 92, 126).

Coming to a sensitive and responsible understanding of the dynamics of parent-teacher partnerships is an evolutionary process. The early childhood years are a time when this understanding can germinate and emerge in a healthy manner. Yet, as is true with all growth-oriented experiences, there are times when conflicts and misunderstandings will occur. These stressors should be seen as opportunities for growth; chances to better articulate our roles and responsibilities toward children and toward each other (9). In this sense, teachers and parents have a responsibility to prompt in each other the thinking through of roles and responsibilities that each needs to be pursuing. For example, teachers in many preschool programs often experience the "late pick-up" syndrome, where parents are not sensitive to the teacher's need for rest and renewal. This is an opportunity to engage parents in rethinking their part in developing a healthy family-school relationship. Likewise, in too many cases, parents have faced situations where teachers are not sensitive to the particular needs of the child. Here, too, is an opportunity for parents to prompt in teachers an assessment of their interactions with children. These are just two examples of the types of growth experiences that often arise in the early involvement of parents and teachers (38, 39).

The initiation of home visits, family centers, group-oriented parent-teacher education programs, community-based family projects, and collaborative family-school problem-solving efforts are ways to promote a context in which an authentic construct of parent-teacher partnerships can emerge (114). The formative years of family life is a time when parents seek out an understanding of their roles through their interactions with helpers such as teachers. In some cases this seeking out takes place in actions that may reflect a lack of knowledge or willingness to take on new challenges. In other cases it may appear in actions that indicate a lack of resources for coping with particular stressors. And in other situations it will appear in actions that reflect parents' positive understanding of their many roles (114). Regardless, it is important for teachers to view these actions as a part of parents' growth in acquiring a better understanding of their role in the partnership.

Ultimately, the most powerful learning that occurs during the early childhood years may well be the learning that goes on between parent and teacher. For it is the parent and teacher roles that carry the most significance for the child's lifelong learning (9, 38, 51, 77, 122). Thus, these years are an opportune time for teachers to initiate and then build partnerships that reflect shared decision making, to encourage parent initiatives regarding their involvement in family and school activities, and to begin the process of shared leadership with parents (9, 18, 20, 40, 48, 62, 91, 98). It is also a time for teachers to sharpen their understanding of the challenges parents confront and to engage with parents in advocacy efforts that can lead to more family-centered policies in the larger society (41, 51, 88, 109).

HANDLING ROLE CONFLICTS

All relationships experience the stress of role conflicts. Indeed, the nature of intense partnerships such as those that take place between parents and teachers require stress points as a means of feedback and stimulus for growth (34, 38, 70, 105, 112). For example, teachers who expect parents to be at every activity may feel stressed as some parents define their participation in more limited ways. This conflict can function as a point of dialogue between teachers and parents on what are desired and realistic expectations for each other's participation. Similar stress is experienced among parents and teachers with regard to many issues such as expectations regarding each other's roles; styles of teaching and parenting; attitudes toward each other; daily activity schedules; curriculum emphases; and expected child behavior (114, 115).

Gordon (44), Powell (92), Swick and Duff (113), and others (15, 80, 97) offer many suggestions on how to use conflict as a means to actually strengthen teacher-parent partnerships. One strategy is to gain insight into each other's cultural orientation and learning philosophy. For example, through informal individual and group discussions, parents and teachers can gain information on how they feel about several issues such as discipline, communication, decision making, and curriculum. Multiple opportunities to share and discuss issues of a mutual concern can prompt ideas on how to resolve issues. Further, insights gleaned from this process can be used to better articulate parent and teacher roles as they take shape within a partnership approach (40, 55, 70, 91). Daily contacts, informal interactions at school and community events, written notes to each other, and other relationship-building interactions are some ways to foster this growth process (113).

Additional strategies include preventive efforts such as role-clarification activities early on in the relationship, periodic support activities such as family-school socials or teacher-parent coffees, and provisions for some mutual learning activities among parents and teachers (114). Resolving role conflicts calls for the use of proven communication strategies including active listening, perspective-taking, responsiveness, reflective dialogue, and the use of problem-solving schemes (34, 55, 56, 71). Conflict resolution occurs best in settings that have a system for continuing communication and that promote a sense of positive support among the participants (114).

CONFRONTATION AS SPRINGBOARD TO LEARNING

Several factors have been noted as influencing the emergence of parent-teacher confrontations: lack of communication, a failure to account for the other person's perceptions or needs, anxiety over one's inability to solve a particular issue, displacement of one's frustration toward others, and disgust over another person's failure to respond to a situation (39, 70, 114). Factors such as these typically lead to a major breakdown in parent-teacher interactions. The breakdown may be perceived or real; in either case the results are indicative of a major stress within the relationship.

Teachers point to the following factors as some of the major sources of stress in parents that they believe are often at the foundation of confrontations: personal trauma, family dysfunction, overload from work and family schedules, lack of support, mental health problems, major value differences with the school, and justifiable concerns about teachers or school situations (117). Parents identify the following as sources of stress in teachers that often lead to confrontations: lack of training, overcrowded classrooms, lack of support, burnout, value differences with the family, and low pay (38). These sources of stress among parents and teachers need to be understood and accounted for in the development of partnership plans.

Two types of confrontation occur most often: the sudden, unexpected outburst of a parent or teacher; and the type of emotional discharge that results from some continuing stressor that has not been resolved. *The immediate task of the teacher is to try, in collaboration with the parent, to locate the source of the problem.* Galinsky provides a problem-solving sequence that teachers and parents can use in transforming confrontation and conflict into productive learning experiences (38, p. 11):

1. *Describe the situation as a problem out in front.* Avoid accusations or the implication that the source of the problem resides in the personality of the parent or the child (or it could be added, the teacher).
2. *Generate multiple solutions.* Parents and professionals should both do this, and no one's suggestions should be ignored, put down, or denounced.
3. *Discuss the pros and cons* of each suggestion.
4. *Come to a consensus* about which solutions to try.
5. *Discuss* how you will implement these solutions.
6. *Agree to meet again* to evaluate how these solutions are working so that you can change your approach, if necessary.

These strategies have proved useful in helping teachers and parents establish a basis for working collaboratively to solve conflicts.

Beyond the urgency of the context of the immediate confrontation is a need for some long-range efforts. Confrontation usually indicates a serious lack of communication and/or neglect of needs that should prompt the partners to develop some long-range plans. For example, there may be a need to better articulate feelings and thoughts related to particular sources of tension. Or, a need may exist to look critically at a broader set of issues that may be influencing parents and teachers in negative ways. From the parental perspective, for example, teacher insensitivity to a child's handicap is cause for alarm. Yet, the teacher may not be aware of all of the complexities of the child's handicap or of the parent's feelings in this regard. In a corresponding fashion, teachers may feel unsupported in their efforts to create in the child a positive orientation toward learning. They may have negative feelings regarding a lack of parent involvement in creating more positive learning attitudes in children. From these stressful feelings many conflicts arise, are temporarily solved, and then emerge again, thus creating a cycle of continuing stress in the partnership (79, 80, 94).

Conflict resolution is based on the willingness of teachers and parents to engage in dialogue regarding the events and perceptions that are at the center of their misunderstandings. Galinsky (38, 39) and Swick (114) note that continuing parent-teacher dialogue (using appropriate planning and problem-solving strategies) has proved successful not only in resolving specific conflicts but also in creating a positive framework for having more productive partnerships. Dialogue regarding conflicts between parents and teachers during the early childhood years often leads to better insights on issues such as the following:

- Appropriate expectations for children as they experience different stages of development.

- Specific family or school situations that influence children's behavior and learning.

- Skills that children need to develop for functioning effectively in group situations.

- Approaches that parents and teachers can use to promote in children (and in themselves) the development of a positive self-image.

- Ideas for improving the family's work and family schedules.

- Plans for having regular communication among parents, teachers, and children.

Some of the factors that comprise various parent-teacher confrontations (e.g., alcoholism, spouse abuse, psychopathologies) are not amenable to immediate resolution. Particular stressors may require long-term solutions such as therapy, rehabilitation, or combinations of strategies that may begin in the school but extend to the use of other helping professionals (12, 115). Other elements that are embedded in the contexts of specific confrontations (class size, cultural misunderstandings, and value conflicts) require a team approach where "third-party" supporters such as school administrators or community leaders become involved in attempting to reshape the contexts toward resolution (30, 31). However, where a collaborative approach is used, significant progress can be made. Through the use of a learning and supportive orientation to resolving confrontations, high regard is nurtured among all of the participants (70, 79, 92). Atkinson (3) notes that much of the anxiety experienced by homeless families relates to the low regard in which they are held by their helpers. This is likely the case with most parents and teachers who experience a lack of support and sense a low-regard feeling from those who are their most likely source of hope.

HIGH REGARD: VALUING EACH OTHER

While most teachers and other helping professionals pay homage to the need for valuing their partnerships with parents, in far too many cases this belief is eroded through a loss of regard for parents. Parents also experience this irony of believing strongly in the value of teachers and yet gradually allowing their alliance with teachers to erode (114, 115). The concept of *high regard* is critical not only to individual teacher-parent relationships, but also to the long-term involvement of parents and teachers in meaningful partnerships. Thus, the development of strong partnerships should be based on high regard. While the idea of regarding each other as valuable and worthy human beings seems simple, the concept is actually inclusive of some complex understandings. Three components of the concept that impinge on parent-teacher partnerships in significant ways are regard for oneself, a sense of mutuality regarding each other's importance and worth, and a human system for nurturing in self and others the value of positive living (9, 68).

Each of these attributes of high regard is discussed in terms of its meaning, its relationship to teacher-parent partnerships, and in relation to ways each can be promoted in parents and teachers. Far too often teacher-parent relationships suffer from a lack of understanding regarding high regard and the role it plays in their development of meaningful and lasting partnerships. Involvement activities, especially those that require planning and decision making never acquire their full value unless a strong sense of regard exists in the partners (115). Where high regard exists, parents and teachers are able to grow through their relationships with each other despite the challenges confronted.

The foundation of high regard is in the self-perception of

each person. One must have high regard for self in order to understand why others desire to be treated with regard. This sense of self-importance cannot be based on an artificial self-image, where the person is only going through the motions of imaging oneself as important. It must be based on observable attributes such as taking care of one's health, developing and pursuing one's interests and talents, nurturing one's mental health, planning for self-renewal time, and fostering in oneself an ongoing image of a growing, learning, and healthy person (7, 9, 37, 60, 66, 72). For example, a parent who has high regard, plans for time alone, pursues interests that promote his/her individual growth, and sees him/herself as worthy (37). Likewise, teachers with high regard develop interests beyond teaching, cherish renewal opportunities, and nurture a sense of worth in themselves (122). Teachers and parents who exhibit attributes reflective of high regard are able to accept and use conflicts and mistakes as opportunities for growth. Individuals lacking in high regard tend to expect too much of others, as if to make up for their low self-esteem. The parent (or teacher) who always sees the other person as the source of difficulty usually is suffering from low regard. Gordon (44) noted dramatic improvements in parent-child relationships as parents increased their sense of regard for themselves. Parent educators (or professionals in this role) need to account for this element of regard in their training and support programs; it is often the most needed element in parent attempts to improve their parenting (44). By way of inference of the data in their work with teachers, Swick and McKnight (122) found that teachers who were involved in personal and professional renewal and who viewed themselves as important persons were more likely to pursue parent-involvement activities.

Evolving from one's regard for self, is the ability to see others as worthy and important. Blazer (9) takes note of the critical role that mutuality plays in the development of each person's sense of faith in others and in oneself. From our earliest life experiences we are dependent upon relationships with others that foster this sense of mutual respect and worth. It is at the core of our being, functioning like a continuing energy source that we give to and take from in a harmonious and yet sometimes stressful manner. It is the part of us that helps us maintain our self-respect in spite of our weaknesses and maintain our respect for others in spite of the differences we may have with them (9, 37, 60). When it is fully developed, this mutuality of regard promotes situations where parents and teachers reach beyond the normal range of functioning to achieve excellence in their partnerships.

When high regard is mutually achieved by teachers and parents, it creates a sense of trust and worth that permeates all of their interactions. Examples of how this process works include situations where parents ask questions before consolidating their judgment on a potential conflict; where teachers reflect on the parents' situation and develop proactive and compassionate ways of relating to it; where parents and teachers carry out continuing rituals of positively reinforcing their valuing of the other person; and where teachers and parents maintain their respect for each other while at the same time attempting to problem solve (3, 20, 62, 73). High regard, as observed in parent-teacher partnerships, acts as a source of strength and growth for parents and teachers (44). For example, it has been observed that when they sensed that teachers valued them as worthy persons, the parents increased their positive regard for teachers. They responded more often to teacher requests, initiated more communication with teachers, and participated more in teacher-sponsored programs at the school (121). It has also been noted in programs attempting to reach adolescent parents that when they sensed that they were valued by home visitors as worthy individuals, they responded more fully to the home visitors' requests (84).

Some of the more notable indicators of relationships that have achieved this sense of mutuality related to high regard include sensitivity to each other's needs and situations; continu-

131

ous communication with each other; going beyond the expected in helping and supporting each other; being responsive to each other's inquiries in an active manner; and participating in proactive activities that enhance each other's self-esteem (22, 37, 92, 101, 111). Beneath these surface indicators is a foundation of individual regard that serves to foster positive partnerships. Stinnett (111) noted this regard in high-support families and in successful family-school relationships. It is more than simply exhibiting behaviors that reflect a respect for others, it is the active commitment of human beings to being the best that they can be, both individually and collaboratively (7, 66).

Clearly, the mutual sense of high regard that makes for truly meaningful and positive teacher-parent partnerships must have a system that enables the partners to foster it. This system, as it has been observed and studied, is much more than a written plan of action; it is an *ecology of caring that permeates the family-school relationship* (23, 40, 44, 62, 93, 96, 115, 126). Prevalent in this ecology are attitudes among staff and parents that reinforce in each other their mutual importance and their significant role in the education of children. Many opportunities exist or are created to promote sharing of feelings, discussion of ideas, solving of problems, and the shaping of new ways to respond to both parent and teacher needs. Committees, study teams, conferences, informal visits, support groups, and many other avenues are used to promote a sense of high regard among parents and teachers (93, 114). High-regard environments reflect modern paradigms in beginning early to engage families and schools in supportive actions and to see each other as the most important elements in the community (20, 32, 93, 114).

CULTURAL DIFFERENCES
AS LEARNING OPPORTUNITIES

In too many cases parent-teacher conflicts are rooted in conflicting and/or distorted cultural perceptions. Lightfoot (70) describes the "worlds apart" syndrome that often permeates family-school interactions. Both teacher and parent misconceptions regarding each other's cultural heritage and values lead to many conflicts. In turn, these conflicts tend to divide parents and teachers, thus impeding the total learning ecology. Such divisive relationships erode children's power to develop healthy self-other images. Further, they foster school and home-learning situations that prohibit the full development of partnerships (2, 16, 26, 70). Three of the most damaging elements of culturally insensitive ecologies are development of incorrect stereotypes, distortion of one's perceptions regarding others' learning capabilities, and the promotion of a "worlds apart" syndrome in parent-teacher relationships.

When people lack a full understanding of another's culture, they tend to rely on stereotypes—images that usually are very incomplete and incorrect (112). Cultural stereotypes arise out of the need for individuals to react to something with which they are insecure; lacking information about an event or person, they thus need an image of how to respond (70). In a gradual, almost subliminal manner, these stereotypes imprison individuals in the mental images and responses they use in relating to others who are different (34, 70).

This form of cultural miseducation has prompted many conflicts and confrontations between families and schools. Consider the bilingual child who is placed in a low reading group but who is reading fluently at home in his native context. Or, consider the child who refuses to embarrass another child by beating him in a race because to do so is antithetical to his/her cultural norms (70). These and other stereotypical responses to children's differences create distrust in the family-school relationship. They engender in children a sense of inadequacy related to school learning and they promote in parents a sense of isolation from the school (34).

Multicultural learning (learning about the values and attributes of other cultures through meaningful and accurate experiences) is the most powerful medium teachers and parents have for promoting strong partnerships. The following multicultural learning strategies have proved effective, especially during the early childhood years:

- Teacher involvement in acquiring accurate and proactive information on the values and attributes of children and parents from different cultures (34).

- Strategies that bring teachers and parents together in warm, supportive interactions where they learn about each other (and their cultural attributes) in positive ways (2).

- Shared teacher-parent learning experiences that broaden their cultural understanding of each other (40).

- Parent-teacher involvement in planning and carrying out classroom learning activities that capitalize on children's cultural diversities as learning strengths (112).

- Family-school events that integrate cultural learning into the substance of the many interactions of children, parents, and teachers (2).

- Family, school, and community education programs that focus on broadening everyone's understanding of the ways people in different cultures live and learn (34).

- Refinement and adaptation of school curricula and instructional practices to reflect a sensitivity to the ways in which different children learn (112).

The continued use of multicultural learning activities is the best antidote to the many misconceptions that often permeate family-school relationships where culturally insensitive stereotypes prevail.

Within the context of cultural distortion, there are many misunderstandings related to how children learn (112). Unfortunately, when people do not understand the learning styles of others, they often see them as inferior to their way of relating to life (70). For example, it is not uncommon for some teachers to unconsciously spend more time with learners who are the least disruptive of their cognitive maps (112). Indeed, in some cases, children's learning differences are seen as deficits. A good example of this misconception is the bilingual child's initial shyness in English-speaking classrooms. While the teacher may see this shyness as a lack of initiative, further assessment will usually reveal that the child is simply adjusting to a new environment, much like adults do when confronted with a totally new situation (34). Another example is that of the second-grade boy who was late to class every day because he was responsible for feeding his bedridden aunt each morning. Afraid to tell his teacher of the situation and not wanting to burden his mother, he suffered much criticism until the teacher visited his mother.

Value differences, situational elements, and divergent learning styles offer parents and teachers many opportunities for shared learning. The following strategies have proved helpful:

- Teacher involvement in getting to know the parents and children on a personal level, becoming familiar with their interests, situations, and values (34).

- Parent-teacher sharing of cultural, family, and school interests and concerns as related to broadening and strengthening their partnership (20).

- Teacher involvement in learning about cultures, learning styles predominant in different cultures, and strategies for accommodating different styles through collaborative home- and school-learning approaches (2, 16, 96).

- Parent involvement in functioning as classroom resource teachers on ethnic and cultural practices (114).

- Teacher-parent orientation, discussion, and information-sharing activities that are scheduled on a regular basis (114).

- Family-school cultural enrichment activities that foster a supportive understanding among teachers and families about the positive aspects of their cultural differences (2, 34).

- Teacher-parent study teams that assess and plan multicultural curriculum experiences in a collaborative manner (20).

The "worlds apart" syndrome that exists in some school-family relationships (70) can be transformed into a "learning relationship" that promotes unity through the integration of cultural differences into the partnership in positive ways. Teacher assessment of their attitudes, skills, and resources (related to planning a multicultural early childhood program) is a first step. The fostering of parent involvement in learning about and contributing to the school's cultural enrichment is another step in this process. Teacher-parent partnership activities that are directed toward enriching the curriculum and each other's perspectives is certain to strengthen children's position for success in school and life (20, 70, 112). Every aspect of the learning environment needs continuous renewal in this regard; curriculum design, instructional materials, teacher perspectives, assessment tools, and—very importantly—the decision-making system. The roots of cultural ignorance are deep in our history and a primary mission of teacher-parent partnerships must be to enlighten themselves and their children regarding the vast riches existent in the cultures of the world (20, 34).

SUPPORTING AT-RISK FAMILIES

The early childhood years are the most amenable time for reaching families who confront serious risks. The concept of risk implies that some form of danger exists to the individual's integrity (27). Further, risks function like stressors in that they require individuals to focus most of their energy on responding to them. While all people face risks, *the concept of "at-risk,"* as it is used in early childhood education, indicates the children/families are in situations that threaten their immediate and long-term well-being (27). These situations have their sources in both constitutional and environmental contexts.

The *at-risk syndrome* can be organized around the categories of severity that are facing children and families. *Low risk* would imply that the child and family is not facing a serious threat; that while there may be one or two risk attributes present, these factors do not represent a serious erosion of integrity. *Moderate risk* implies that two or more risk attributes are present and represent a distinct threat or potential danger to the child and family. *High risk* indicates that the child and family are experiencing events that place their integrity and functioning at risk (115). Children and families in the highest risk category usually confront multiple risk conditions that combine to act as a debilitating influence on their lives. For example, homeless families are often experiencing many events beyond, and yet interrelated, to homelessness: poverty, illiteracy, desertion, unemployment, poor health care, and a myriad of related factors (3, 26).

Left unchecked, risk factors may well contribute to the family's deterioration and to the child's failure in school. Early childhood teacher-parent partnerships can play a major role in

137

preventing high-risk child and family situations from emerging as well as a substantive role in resolving risk conditions that already exist (12, 72, 91, 121). As briefly described earlier, multidimensional early intervention programs are proving effective in reducing the risks families confront. There are several strategies that partnership efforts can promote in this regard. For example:

- Teacher-parent involvement in promoting community awareness of risk factors that typically threaten young families (27).

- Teacher acquisition of knowledge and skills for effectively responding to the needs of at-risk children and parents (6, 115).

- Parent involvement in training and educational programs that focus on strengthening their parenting skills (40).

- Teacher involvement in preschool parent-oriented education and support activities that promote the prevention of at-riskness in children and families (32).

- Parent-teacher involvement in support activities that strengthen the family-school-community network of preventive services for young children and their parents (40).

- Teacher networking with human services professionals on resources, services, and activities that can be used to prevent and/or resolve at-risk conditions that threaten children and families (2).

- Parent-teacher involvement in planning and implementing home- and school-based programs that support parents and children in achieving school success (121).

In developing partnerships with at-risk parents, teachers need to attend to several skills and strategies: *awareness* of the multiple risks that parents of young children may experience; *insight* into the dynamics of how at-riskness influences the lives of parents and children; *understanding* of the specific at-risk parent-child situations that exist in their classroom; *sensitivity* to the feelings and position of at-risk parents; *strategies* that are particularly relevant to the involvement and support of at-risk parents; *alliances* with formal and informal professional and community resources for use in support of at-risk parents; and a *communication system* with at-risk parents that facilitates their development as well as that of their children (3, 23, 70, 72, 121).

Teacher awareness of the countless risks that confront parents is a powerful antidote to their formation of incorrect stereotypes. Through workshops, professional reading, courses, and other avenues teachers can, along with self-reflection, acquire authentic images of the complexities of various risk conditions. For example, an insightful assessment of homelessness reveals several facts: families with children under six are rapidly becoming a significant part of this subpopulation (27); homelessness is not restricted to the poor (3); children who are homeless do well in school when their insecurities are addressed (26); and a growing percentage of homeless adults are employed (3). Yet these facts about homeless people are not the substance of the stereotype of homelessness that most people hold (27). Similar problems exist regarding people's perceptions of poverty, illiteracy, and other risk factors. For example, in spite of poverty, many children are successful in school when they have high support from their parents and teachers (16). The following is a list of risk factors prevalent during the early childhood years that need to be understood within the unique context of each family.

Risk Factors Often Faced by Parents and Children

Poverty
Illiteracy
Malnutrition
Alcohol/Drug Abuse
Family Pathologies
Poor Health Care
Low Support Resources
Unemployment

It is critical to recognize that while these risk factors affect the lives of many families, they do not eliminate the innate goodness of each child and parent affected. Teacher awareness of the strengths of at-risk families is essential to their avoiding the stereotyping of families who confront even the most serious problems in negative ways.

The influence of different risk factors on the functioning of parents and children needs to be fully conceived as teachers need an understanding of the dynamics of "riskness" as it relates to their partnership efforts with families. In high-risk families, for example, multiple risk factors that occur in intensive and chronic ways appear to encourage conditions in the person and in his/her ecology that erode their integrity (115). The lack of resources and skills, poverty, illiteracy, and poor health tend to reduce one's ability to respond effectively to stress (27). Most teachers have had experiences where this integrity-erosion process has negatively influenced their own behavior (38). For example, overcrowded classrooms, lack of resources, and low support can erode teachers' ability to cope with stress (122). This same process is at work in high-risk parents and can become so powerful that it creates a family context that promotes intergenerational powerlessness (101). When this process is at work during the family's initial development, it can be devastating. An example is Karen, a 17-year-old new parent.

At age 15 Karen left home to avoid being sexually abused by her father. Soon she was in with a drug crowd, then dropped out of school, and eventually became pregnant. She is not sure who the baby's father is, is not welcome to return home, and is fearful of what juvenile authorities will do to her.

In cases such as Karen's, only intensive and highly supportive intervention will serve to guide her toward a more healthy and productive life-style. Karen needs a support network, literacy skills, counseling, parent education, services for her baby, and many other resources in order to prevent the development of serious pathologies (12).

An extension of teacher insights on the dynamics of various family risks is their full understanding of the specific risk situations of the parents and children in their classrooms (115). The real damage of teacher ignorance about the risk context of their children and parents is twofold: it isolates them from having authentic helping relationships; and it reinforces the low self-image and powerless feelings in the very children and parents who need empowering relationships the most (115). What is needed is teachers' involvement in becoming fully aware of the family's context so that they can relate their program to the family in a supportive way. Swick (115) provides five areas of teacher focus related to their learning about the at-risk families in their classrooms:

1. What are the risk factors specifically present in the family?

2. What are the underlying sources of these factors?

3. How are the risk factors present in the family influencing their functioning both within the family and in the school?

4. What are some family strengths that can be high-lighted for pursuing a positive partnership effort?

5. How can the teacher become more supportive of the

141

parents and children in the classroom who are at risk?

A significant factor in becoming knowledgeable about families' risk situations is the teacher's sensitivity to the position in which at-risk parents and children find themselves (23, 34, 43, 57, 70). Having experienced tremendous stress, possible abuse, and various forms of degradation, high-risk parents and children often feel helpless, exuding a sense of anxiety about possibly experiencing even more stress (115). While reactions may vary (from very passive to extremely agressive), the core feelings of anger, distrust, shame, doubt, and anxiety are common among high-risk families. Teacher sensitivity to these feelings, as they actually occur in at-risk families, is critical to understanding that these parents and children not only need major support but also need empowerment related to their self-image (86, 91). Respect for their unique situations is an essential beginning point for having meaningful relationships with at-risk parents and children.

Home visits, informal discussions, special assistance activities, and mutually developed ideas on responding to particular risks are strategies teachers have found to be responsive to the unique situations of at-risk families. Powell (92) notes that in many cases parents tend to reveal their concerns more in informal, confidential settings. As these situations are handled with respect, dignity, and confidentiality by teachers, parents gain the needed trust for building productive relationships (117). The recent work of Nichols (82) and Atkinson (3) deserves special mention as both are engaged in innovative parent-oriented at-risk prevention projects. Nichols (82), for example, is working with high-risk families from an intensive, multiple-strategies perspective. She is attempting to empower parents (and their children) who have experienced abusive and/or degrading circumstances before pathologies take root in the family. Utilizing a very personable and supportive environment (The Nurturing Center) combined with an individualized plan for

142

each family (developed by the parent in collaboration with the helper), parents are engaged in activities that aim to strengthen them and their children. Family play therapy, counseling, parent support groups, parent education, adult literacy, social services resources, and health care resources are some of the strategies that are being explored in this exemplary project (82).

Atkinson (3) is using a similar design with emphasis on providing homeless families with quality child care (birth–5 years of age) the initial point of contact and interaction. Interrelated with the child care, however, are several services that engage parents in strengthening their position as family leaders: self-image building, housing, health care, adult literacy and job training, and parent education (3). Both programs are based on the empathetic, empowerment concept, building on existing parental strengths and focusing on positive ways that families can strengthen themselves further. They create partnerships with parents that are based on mutual respect, trust, and compassion.

Finally, in working with moderate- and high-risk parents in an especially designed early childhood teacher-parent partnership program, Swick (121) found that highly individualized and person-oriented strategies were most effective in gaining the involvement of the parent at risk (121). It was especially evident that well-trained home visitors were successful in involving moderately at-risk parents in regular partnership activities with their children's teachers. They were also successful in engaging high-risk parents in intervention services and activities that strengthened their status to resolve some of the problems they were confronting. Individual and small-group activities proved most effective in reaching parents who were involved in the program (121).

The work of Atkinson (3), Nichols (82), Swick (121), and others (11, 12, 52, 63, 69, 77, 84, 86, 92, 98, 111) indicates that school-family-community alliances are vital to the prevention or resolution of the issues confronted by at-risk families. Beyond the essential formal alliances with support agencies are alliances with significant helpers in the community that may have particular resources and supports that engage at-risk families in building a structure for a more positive future. For example, Powell (92) observed that parents seem to thrive on communication and feedback from other parents and friends who are experiencing events similar to theirs. Swick (121) found success with utilizing paraprofessional mentors (who were often neighbors or friends of the parents) in helping at-risk parents link up to the more formal support groups in the community. Indeed, case management theory is encouraging an empathetic, comprehensive approach to engaging parents in activities that strengthen their total status as individuals and as family leaders (23). The successful "alliance-oriented" child-care program for homeless families guided by Atkinson includes several points that are applicable to partnership efforts that focus on at-risk parents (3, p. 3):

Involve parents in developing their plan of needs and ways to meet these needs.

Become personally familiar with agencies and support groups who are to be used in your alliance of helpers.

While utilizing the components of case management, individualize and humanize this process to promote in parents a positive self-image.

Be a true partner with parents; assist them in dealing with the stress that often comes when using an agency or support group.

Continually assess how parents' "network of helpers" is influencing them and their children.

The essential element in successful partnerships with at-risk families is the communication process (115). Far too often teachers use a directed, authority-based form of communicating with parents (114). While such a form of communication is ineffective with parents in general, it is disastrous with at-risk parents. Highly formal, authoritative communication too often lacks the two major components vital to involving at-risk parents in meaningful partnerships: *closeness* and *mutuality* (9). Parents under heavy stress need the closeness that exists in responsive, supportive, and sensitive communication. They also need a feeling of mutuality, a sense of togetherness with significant others as they attempt to resolve problems and stressors (11, 86). In attempting to create an inviting communication environment, teachers have found the following strategies and ideas to be useful:

- Involve parents in "investing" part of themselves in the environment by making learning materials, helping with classroom tasks, and through other contributions (82).

- Learn about the strengths and needs of the parents; know them in a human way (3).

- Be a good role model; respond sensitively to the needs of the children and parents you serve (115).

- Focus on parent involvement from a partnership orientation, taking into account the various perspectives of parents (18).

- Listen actively to parental issues, concerns, and views; attempt to see things from their point of view.

At-risk families need more than the usual support resources and they need tremendous focusing on the development of positive self-images. Teacher-parent partnerships involving at-risk families have found success when the partnership responds first to their special needs, their context, and their need to see themselves as capable, worthy people. Without such a foundation, little can be accomplished with regard to other aspects of the partnership.

Chapter 7

TEACHER-PARENT PARTNERSHIPS FOR STRONG CHILDREN AND FAMILIES

In a global society that requires a high level of literacy and a sophisticated level of social competence, children and families confront unprecedented experiences. These experiences include the need for more education, a new understanding of what makes people humane, and a sensitivity to the complexities of living in a constantly changing world. In facing the challenges inherent in these experiences it is clear that families must have a strong foundation and meaningful alliances, with their helpers in the community. The lack of such alliances, along with a deterioration of the value and context of parenting, has prompted severe stress in today's families, especially in families who are just beginning to cope with the challenges of the early childhood years (11).

The fallout from stressors such as economic deprivation, social isolation, and illiteracy has been dramatic as indicated by marked increments in divorce, family abuse, single-parent families, and family mental health problems (14, 27). These family stress-related problems are interrelated with many of the issues of children's failure to benefit from school: poor health, lack of literacy tools, mental health problems, and other such indicators (41). Naturally, these negative behavior indicators have a far-reaching influence on our entire society.

In effect, the challenges confronting families are, in the microcosm, the very issues that threaten the fabric of the society. Illiteracy, poverty, crime, abuse, and related pathologies eventually erode a society's integrity and promulgate additional stressors. While the formation of strong teacher-parent partnerships during the early childhood years will not resolve all of the stressors inherent in the revolution our world is experiencing, they will significantly influence the foundation of two of the society's most critical human ecologies: the family and the school (115). The creation of such partnerships call for a family-school agenda that focuses on five elements: the articulation of a new construct of parenting and teaching that is relevant to the challenges now facing families and schools; the formation of a system by which parents and teachers can initiate their partnerships during the earliest period of the family's life; a restructuring of school ecologies toward a "family involvement" model of education; the development of early childhood school-community alliances that are truly oriented toward promoting strong families and children; and the creation of public policies that will undergird the need for a stronger family-school relationship (1, 20, 32, 40, 51, 92, 98, 121). While these five elements have received attention throughout this book, this synthesis and elaboration provides a clear vision for families and schools as they reach toward strengthening themselves and their children's future.

PARENTING AND TEACHING: FACING THE CHALLENGES

Whenever dramatic social change occurs, society's basic leaders are challenged to find new ways of functioning. This is certainly the case for parents and teachers, where change is begging for both a strengthening of roles that historically have sustained families and schools, and for developing new ways of carrying out these roles in response to a changed environment (2, 92, 96). For example, with the stressors inherent in our more complex society, it is vital that parents attend to the critical roles of nurturing, guiding, and modeling. Yet it is also important that parents explore new ways of carrying out these roles (115). Given that parents indeed need more skills, time, and resources to effectively negotiate their roles, it is critical that they not only see themselves in a leadership situation but that the larger society also views them as important and provides them with the supportive resources needed (41, 86).

The construct of parenting that needs to emerge is one where parents are viewed as family leaders, as individuals who are intimately engaged in helping their children (and themselves) become fully competent. In this perspective, parents are expected to focus on their primary mission of "family building" as well as to be involved in the process of linking the family to the community in productive ways. This view of parenting calls for support structures that emphasize an education for parenthood that encourages parents to acquire an image (and the needed skills) for becoming individuals who grow through parenthood. In this sense, parenting is seen as a *covenant* with the community that seeks to promote healthy children and strong families (9).

Likewise, teaching needs to be revisioned as a covenant with families and the society that is primarily focused on supporting the development of competent human beings (20, 40, 115). In restructuring the teaching paradigm, three contextual issues need close attention: validation, training, and support for a cadre of highly paid teacher/caregivers for the preschool years; redesign of the focus of training early childhood teachers' experience toward a family-focused program; and a refinement in the role-structure system that places the emphasis on the "educator" and "caregiver" aspects of early childhood as opposed to the more limited construct of "teacher" (115).

In the role of educator, teachers of young children need to "image" themselves as guides, teachers, and role models who are designing and managing learning ecologies that promote humane and growth-oriented practices in children and their parents. This enlarged and more responsive vision of teaching must also be grounded within the total system, inclusive of home, school, community and the larger society (32). It is especially important that early childhood educators include these systems in their planning and teaching because research clearly indicates that single-dimension (child only) programs have a very limited reach (105). Further, research (6, 22, 93) indicates that the most effective teaching approach in early childhood is one that emphasizes a guiding, responsive, and nurturing style rather than a directive, imparting, and authority-based style.

The appropriate paradigm for early childhood teachers is one in which they see themselves as "in covenant" with the entire family for achieving human competence in a shared, sensitive, and compassionate manner (9). And, in the pursuit of this covenant, families are seen as arenas of strength and potential greatness rather than as arenas of weakness and potential disaster.

MAKING PARTNERSHIPS POSSIBLE: ELEMENTS OF A NEW DESIGN

In all of the work on school reform, the most substantive focus has been on creating a new system by which the key adult partners in the learning process can develop and sustain a meaningful covenant (31, 62, 95). The most significant observation about this needed restructuring is the emphasis on beginning the partnership process as early in the family's life as is feasible. Learning about the skills needed for functioning in shared relationships cannot wait until the formal school years. By the time children reach kindergarten, parents have already developed the behavior patterns they use in various relationship settings (104). The case is the same for teachers in that their concepts of parent involvement typically are formed during their early experiences in teaching. Two needed design elements emerge from this perspective: *initiate parent-teacher partnerships during the preschool years, and engage parents and teachers in training situations* where they can acquire skills and perspectives for carrying out meaningful relationships with each other (113, 114, 115).

In order to carry out these elements, the structure in which families and schools function must be changed. A brief assessment of the current ways that parents and teachers function (especially as related to the contexts in which they operate) is enlightening with regard to some of the needed changes. Beyond the efforts of a few innovative early childhood family-oriented programs, there are few attempts to create a life-span paradigm regarding family-school relationships. For example, typically parents see their role as confined to the basic maintenance of child and family needs during the preschool years, carrying out what efforts they can to assure the family's well-being. Teachers tend to define their identity within the immediate descriptors of their teaching position (e.g., "I teach 4's" or "I teach first grade"). Further, most school and community leaders perceive the school's beginning point with kindergarten (in some cases including 4-year-old child development). This observation is not meant to be a negative commentary on this situation, but rather to indicate the needed rethinking of the structure by which teachers and parents become engaged (15).

This rethinking needs to include several components: a redefinition of the family and the school's role in children's learning; a revision of how early childhood educators are trained; the development of a structure by which relationships are initiated early in the family's life; inclusion of parent education material related to the parents' role in family-school partnerships; and an extension of these components into the comprehensive school system. Essential to the success of this restructuring is a reformulation of how schools are staffed and how they function (126).

Redefining the family and the school's role in children's learning should emerge from the research that clearly shows the significance of having capable adults intimately involved in children's development from birth. This intimate involvement can occur (as in programs such as Parents as Teachers) through parent-child interactions that are guided and supported by parent educators (who might reside in schools). Further, such a structure would include a comprehensive team of family helpers in the areas of health, counseling, education, and related areas (115). It is important that this structure be legitimized within the school's policy-making system, and that it is funded as an important element of the total educational program (51). This design also requires that schools and local child-care centers form partnerships to facilitate this structure that supports early family-school relationships.

Training of early childhood educators must be refocused on promoting in teacher/caregivers a family-centered approach (105, 113, 114). This refocusing should include training components that provide teachers with skills in home visiting, parent education, interagency collaboration, family life content, teacher-parent partnership skills, and related family-centered skills (114). While these training components do exist in bits and pieces in many early childhood teacher education programs, they too often are ignored with emphases going mostly to classroom strategies and skills. Further, family-centered practices need to be integrated into teacher practices throughout the early childhood years; too often they receive less attention with the initiation of the formal school years (105).

Early childhood education programs need to be organized so that family-school partnerships begin at birth and continue throughout the early years of life. This organizational system might include particular outcomes desired for the family and the school to achieve for each year of the child's life. For example, a goal for the first year of life could be that a parent educator works monthly with the family on appropriate developmental learning activities, supports the family in acquiring needed health and social services, and functions as a bridge for the family in helping them to link up with needed community and school resources (22, 23, 32, 114). Inclusive in this new organizational pattern must be "check-points" where the family and the school can take stock of how their partnership is working, exploring the growth process as it is taking shape in children, parents, and teachers. Vital to the effectiveness of this process is the involvement of parents in decision-making activities where they take on the primary role of educators of their children during these critical years. As this organizational scheme is created, it must be integrated throughout the entire early childhood program so that, for example, primary grade teachers consider the family as the key point in the learning process (105).

Parents also need information and support in reshaping their perceptions of their role in children's learning and development. While early childhood parent education programs have achieved an enviable record in providing parents with information on parenting, child development, and related topics, similar achievements need to be attained in helping parents articulate a more comprehensive identity as related to their role in children's learning. In far too many cases, parents see teaching and learning as processes that occur primarily in schools. This incorrect stereotype has indeed negatively influenced the lives of many children and parents. Parent education content on the roles of nurturing, teaching, and modeling (as they occur within the parent-child relationship) is critical to parental conceptions of their role in children's learning. Further, content on parental roles in linking the family to the school and community (roles such as collaboration, problem solving, and decision making) is needed to fully promote a quality learning setting for everyone in the family (1, 20, 31, 40, 105).

Finally, the elements used to restructure early childhood programs toward a family-centered paradigm must also permeate the entire fabric of school systems. Innovative efforts and strategies suggested by Davies (22) and Rich (96) offer "beginning points" that schools can use in restructuring themselves so that parents and teachers are in continuous partnership, working with each other to create success-oriented learning designs for children that extend throughout the school years (22). In attempting to achieve this family-centered structure, schools will need to create professional and paraprofessional roles that assure the achievement of the goals of this design.

STRUCTURING SCHOOLS FOR SUPPORTING HEALTHY FAMILY DEVELOPMENT

While early childhood educators provide the natural beginning point for establishing a partnership paradigm with families, schools need a structure that is supportive of this effort throughout the entire education system. The elements that comprise a family-centered early childhood program also can serve as a starting point for developing a curriculum for families that supports parents and children in their efforts to achieve success not only in school but also in the broader community arena. In this restructuring, schools should give attention to the elements previously mentioned: early partnership contacts with families, training teachers to work more effectively with families, linking up with other community groups that work with families, and reshaping the program to better reflect families' needs. These elements should be the accepted beginning point for the needed restructuring. In addition, schools should seek to create structures that address the following: helping parents sense that they are needed and wanted as full partners; involving parents in educational experiences that address their parenting and personal needs; supporting families in developing healthy ways of living; providing resources and supports that address the special needs of families; and integrating into the curriculum and instructional process content and strategies that promote learning exchanges between families and schools (19, 22, 62).

In effect, educators need to refocus their orientation to "think family" as opposed to limiting our vision to the children we teach. This philosophical reorientation necessarily will involve school leaders, teachers, and citizens in developing new ways of seeing the role of the school. Critical to any family-centered structure is the thinking of professionals and others who carry out the practices that will support it. School leaders, for example, must model family involvement practices within the context of their roles, especially regarding the policies and decisions made relevant to fostering a more family-oriented program (20). In far too many cases, decisions are made to support single-dimension innovations such as year-round schools without thought given to the impact of such practices on the fabric of the learning teams (parents-children-teachers). On a smaller, yet just as significant scale, are the decisions that unconsciously isolate parents from school involvement such as scheduling conference times that clearly conflict with parental work schedules (114).

In thinking "family-centered," schools must first reorganize themselves around a philosophical premise that places the roles of the family at the center of their decision making. School must be seen as an extended family support rather than as a human sorting mechanism. In attending to this paradigm of the school as a significant part of the family's extended community network, decisions need to be made in light of the following issues and questions:

- Who are the families we serve? What do we know about the parents and children who are a part of our schools? What are their needs, interests, talents, strengths?

- What do we know about ourselves as professional educators? How are we organized, trained, philosophically oriented, and structured? Are we skilled in "thinking family" in relation to the program decisions we make?

- What are our schools like? Are they clean, safe, indicative of active learning, inviting to children and parents, and organized around a family-involvement theme?

- Do we have programs that reflect a "family-centered" school such as child development, parent education, family centers, extended-day enrichment programs, flexible conference scheduling, and "curriculum for caring" teaching practices?

- How are school decisions made? Are parents and teachers intimately involved in collaborative decision making at the building level? Are parents, teachers, and citizens involved in shaping school policies at the district level?

- What practices exist that reflect an ongoing belief in parent-teacher partnerships: parent resource programs, teacher-parent communication, "parent rooms," parents as tutors practices, home-learning projects, parent education programs, and other such activities?

- How is the curriculum and instruction process structured and implemented? Are curriculum resources and practices reflective of family involvement? Are instructional strategies reflective of a family-school learning partnership?

Rich's (95, 96, 98) premise that schools need to be arenas where parents and teachers are building an environment in which home learning is used in collaboration with school learning to build productive lifelong learners is paramount in this family-centered paradigm. Three elements of this focus to support the development of positive lifelong learning habits in children are intimate school-family interaction and planning, the creation of a school-family "curriculum for caring," and the extension of this school-family orientation into the community (114, 115).

Schools need to become intimately involved with families in the planning and nurturing of healthy learning environments. Until

155

recently, isolation may well have been the best descriptor of how schools functioned. Few significant signs of the needed linkages between families and schools existed. Culturally, socially, intellectually, and emotionally, schools too often functioned as islands unto themselves. Beginning with the earliest years of the child's life, parents and educators should be interacting, supporting, planning, assessing, and acting in collaboration with each other to create healthy places and systems in which all members of the family-school team can learn (115). Benchmarks of family-centered schools of today and tomorrow will be parent-teacher planning teams, parent-teacher teaching teams, family-centered places and activities within schools, and an intimacy among parents and teachers that reflects their common covenant to create success-oriented learning environments (9, 20, 115).

In carrying out this covenant, a family-centered "curriculum for caring" must permeate the instructional and social ecologies of the family and the school (9, 40, 48, 88, 92, 115). Such a curriculum needs to address the issues involved in what makes human beings "human" and how we can promote prosocial behaviors in all members of the learning team (66). Through the use of teacher training, leadership renewal, parent education, and citizen support, the key social skills for creating a nurturing environment can be pursued. These include positive self-image, prosocial relationships with others, development of multicultural understandings, sensitive and empathetic relationships, nurturing and positive discipline practices, creative problem-solving strategies, continual dialogue among learners, and other proactive, caring practices (100, 111).

To fully articulate a family-centered orientation, school practices that nurture and support this paradigm need to be interrelated with the community (9). In effect, a human network of family, school, and community learners need to be partners in a covenant for creating positive human environments. In particular, intergenerational teaching/learning teams can provide support for extending school learning through field trips, exchange programs, classroom presentations, tutoring, and participating in school improvement activities (51, 56). Local business, government, and civic groups can provide arenas for children, teachers, and parents to explore applications of skills and extensions of caring through internships, volunteer activities, and joint cultural and social projects.

ALLIANCES FOR STRENGTHENING FAMILIES AND SCHOOLS

Research on how individuals and groups learn and develop in healthy ways strongly indicates that effective human functioning requires a strong support system. This is certainly true with regard to school-family partnerships. Any partnership is, by its very nature, connected to other human systems. Families and schools do not and cannot function in isolation from the community (109). They must have alliances with various community groups in order to carry out their mission and to relate that mission to the goals of the broader society. Indeed, families and schools may, and often do, provide the larger society with new ideas, new directions, and with sources of continuing cultural, social, and economic renewal (102). In this sense, family-school systems must have a healthy stress relationship with the community. Here again, isolation of the systems (family, school, community) creates negative stressors (crime, illiteracy, poverty) on all of the systems. Family/school/community alliances make sense with regard to all of the elements needed for creating a productive and healthy society (102).

In particular, communities need to be in covenant with families and schools regarding the mission of creating learning environments where children can grow and succeed. Everyone in the community needs to see the education and well-being of children and families as their priority; schools must not be challenged to handle this role in isolation from the very sources it serves. There are many natural linkages between what goes on in families and schools and the community: learning, work, leisure, social planning, human development, and all of the dynamics that emerge from these events and experiences (109). There are also many community services that have a natural connection to schools and families: health, social support, economic development, spiritual nurturance, cultural enrichment, and information sharing. These services and processes must be interrelated with what happens in families and schools in ways that promote a prosocial life-style as the community's top priority.

Communities can provide three very valuable contexts for creating productive alliances with families and schools: service, support, and collaborative learning (20, 22, 114). In service contexts, alliances can be created through partnerships that provide health care, family counseling, education, safe neighborhoods, sources of spiritual and social growth, job training, and other services that strengthen families and schools. While these services exist in some form in most communities, they are often provided in isolation from what and how families and schools function. Alliances are needed that relate such services to the needs and interests of parents, children, and teachers, especially during the early childhood years when they can serve as points of growth for those in critical need (115). Interagency teams provide one avenue by which these alliances might occur. The substance of these alliances should be on relating the various needed human services to the strengthening of families and schools. Comprehensive, multidimensional family-oriented programs provide one existing model of how such alliances might be structured (92).

Community support contexts are emerging in the form of school-business partnerships, cooperative school/work programs, school advisory teams, school-community improvement projects, and other meaningful alliances (22). These efforts are needed to provide families and schools with a supportive arena in which they can learn and grow. New supports are needed in the form of collaborative efforts to enable parents to have "family development time" and for parents and teachers to have "partnership time" (40). Further, alliances are needed in which families/schools/communities collaborate as planners and learners in seeking to strengthen the community's fabric for living. Such alliances have to focus on needs as they are reflected in the way of life in the community. Such needs likely will include social, economic, and educational areas of concern. With the help of community leaders, families and schools can address these needs, strengthen their partnership, and promote success-oriented programs for children (20, 40, 109, 114).

SHAPING PUBLIC POLICY
FOR STRONG FAMILIES AND SCHOOLS

While the relationship between the various sectors of any society are complex, there is now a clear indication that public policy and public domain actions strongly influence how families and schools carry out their work (51). A few examples from the past on how policies influence families helps to highlight this relationship. Childhood immunization against life-threatening diseases, which is dependent upon public support, tends to respond to the value placed on it by public policymakers. This has occurred through financial and resource support, and through large-scale educational efforts (27). When funding for immunization is reduced, an increase in particular childhood diseases is observed; likewise, when funding and related support resources are increased, a decrease in these diseases is noticed. Education also plays a key role; with public domain alerts and local educational efforts increased, the problem has been successfully addressed. Life-threatening diseases not only negatively influence the family's well-being, but they also have a detrimental effect on society's social and economic fabric (27, 86).

Another example, specific to the early childhood years, is that of public involvement in promoting quality child care. Where public policy (examples can be seen at local, state, and federal levels) promotes adequate licensing standards, supports the development of quality programs, and advocates for family-centered child-care centers, the results have been encouraging (27). Where efforts to promote appropriate early childhood programs have been minimal or nonexistent, the results have been likewise. In child-care situations where staff are poorly paid, inadequately trained, and lack needed resources, the family and the school are negatively influenced (86).

While the relationship between public policy and family/school outcomes is not totally clear, it is evident that policymakers need to be involved in promoting the exploration of strategies that hold promise for strengthening these arenas of human development and learning. This is particularly the case with support strategies that promote in parents and teachers a stronger sense of control over their lives with regard to bringing them into positive relationships with each other and their community (27, 31, 62, 111). The challenge of negotiating the family's developmental needs within a complex society such as ours requires a high level of support and information so that parents and teachers can maximize their efforts to nurture children toward success. Areas that have emerged as needing special attention in the public domain include, for example, health care, child care, safety, literacy needs, economic resources, family development time, and related areas such as the media exposure children experience (115). A "hands-off" policy in the public domain in regard to these family/school issues is and has been an inhibiting if not degrading influence on the lives of children, parents, and teachers. Just as our nation engages in economic, military, and physical infrastructure planning on a continuing basis, so it must also engage in the ongoing study and planning of improving the family/school infrastructure (27).

An involved citizenry can influence policymakers to consider ways to strengthen families and schools. Parents and teachers, as part of their partnership, need to engage in advocacy efforts that promote public values that are empathetic to change the "human system" toward more responsive practices—actions and means that support healthy family/school relationships (51). This calls for the continuing representation of parents and teachers on school boards, city councils, and through various means at the state and federal levels. In addition, parent-teacher involvement in church, business, civic, and other policy-influencing groups should become part of a system for bringing about an intimate covenant that fosters a new, stronger, and healthier family-school-community environment (9, 22, 40).

Specific needs and issues that require urgent attention related to strengthening young families include improved, affordable, and accessible health care; policies that support family time, especially during the very early years of the family's development; community-centered mental health practices and resources that emphasize preventive strategies during the early childhood years; affordable and quality child/family care and support centers; family friendly workplaces; inviting schools and safe and healthy communities (22, 41, 66, 115). Preventive health care is one of the most effective ways to strengthen families at the very beginning of their journey. Yet, in many cases needed health care resources are either lacking, unaffordable, or difficult to access (27).

Likewise, it is now known that healthy families need time to shape their identity and to nurture each other toward positive and productive ways of living. This need (clearly shown by the dramatic drop in time spent together by parents and children since 1950) calls for major shifts in how families are allowed to function and indeed, how they spend time together. It is both a quality and a quantity issue that is interrelated with all of our society's values (37, 40). Not only are practices such as extended paternity/maternity leave and flexi-scheduling needed, but also there is a need to correlate these practices with family education on the value and role of attachment and nurturing-building rituals in the family's development. How time is spent together is just as important as what time is spent together. Parent education programs need to utilize parent-centered strategies such as parent-peers and parent-directed discussions as ways of engaging families in thinking and planning for family-building time and experiences (110, 111). Further, parent educators, teachers, and parents need to engage community leaders in dialogue that centers on their altering the community's structure to support this needed family time (111, 115).

The challenges today's young families confront require the use of both preventive and problem-solving mental health resources. A crisis exists in this regard as our mental health system is primarily geared toward rehabilitation, not prevention. Stressors such as family-work role and schedule conflicts, family dynamics in an electronic world, environmental stressors such as high-crime areas, and the leadership complexities that influence marital dynamics, require new mental health resources at the local community level (9, 12, 27, 43, 60, 68, 106). Another quantity/quality issue is that of reframing child care into a system that is focused on child/family dynamics that expands to reach all young families during the preschool years (48, 51, 59, 62, 72). These centers of caring and learning must be staffed by capable and sensitive people and must be organized around the needs of the entire family. They need to reach beyond being "ware-houses" to become integral parts of a family-community covenant that includes parent education, parent presence in the classrooms, family support practices, collaboration with business and industry, and the use of intergenerational resource people (40). These should be the most caring places in the society beyond the family's own center of nurturance.

Family-supportive workplaces and safe and nurturing

communities function like a hidden but powerful web of security and meaning for families and schools. How much of young children's hyperactive behavior is really no more than symptomatic of a community that is overcharged with crime, noise pollution, poverty, illiteracy, and other antihuman practices? Families and schools need to be part of a web that is fully connected; responsive to the emotional, social, and spiritual needs of people (102). Cold and unresponsive ecologies are the seedbed of apathy, cynicism, and distrust. Research suggests, for example, that workplace supports such as on-site child care, family sick leave, adequate benefits, enrichment programs, and other nurturing practices not only strengthen families but also improve work performance (114, 115). A similar outcome takes shape in family-oriented communities where safety, recreational, educational, and health resources are integrated with the family and school's efforts. In speaking of this need for total societal effort to support a more human and humane system (especially in regard to health and well-being), Sagan states:

> The unit of health must be broadened beyond the individual to include the entire social network on which the health of the individual depends; a healthy nation is more than a collection of healthy individuals. (102, p. 202)

Schools also need a public policy system that promotes their ability to function as centers of family learning. Resources are needed to encourage school practices that support a family involvement program. Funding should be directed to reshaping early childhood programs toward more emphasis on school-sponsored birth to three years of age family-based projects; interagency-designed parent education activities; quality preschool child development programs; adult literacy courses (with more emphasis on nonformal delivery systems); school-family planning and study teams; school-business cooperative resource and improvement projects; and school-community integration of education with other human services functions (22). Three

163

dimensions of this restructuring process need major attention: intraschool reorganization, school-family partnership training, and communitywide realignment of the elements that critically influence family and school missions. Each dimension, of course, involves many intricate components that will need continuous study and exploration over the next decade. The purpose here is to provide some of the key directions these family-school support efforts need to address.

While school restructuring has gained many vocal adherents, few people have given serious thought to the core of this vital need: *organization of the school ecology so that a viable family-school relationship can be attained* (30, 31, 32). There are many roadblocks within the current structure of schools that preclude the authentic pursuit of teacher-parent partnerships: time, physical structure, staff organization, training, remnants of an irrelevant philosophy, isolationism of teachers, lack of resources, and other truly limiting factors (70, 80, 114). For example, the combination of the traditional one-classroom teacher (isolated from other teachers), along with little or no planning and communication time, clearly create antiparent involvement structures. And with hardly enough resources to handle classroom learning needs, teachers find themselves in a double-bind when it comes to supporting parent-involvement needs. Lack of training, poor leadership, and a static school ecology all tend to push parent involvement toward the back of the priority list (114).

Several components that have proved worth further experimentation with regard to forming meaningful teacher-parent partnerships should be explored within schools: creation of professional/paraprofessional school-family learning teams, planning and use of teaching teams, development of teacher-parent planning times (with scheduled times provided for teacher), teacher involvement in parent-involvement training, schoolwide school/family assessment of the climate for partnerships, planning family-learning environments, parent-teacher leadership training for the entire school staff, and staff-developed plans for restructuring teacher and school practices toward a partnership philosophy (31, 97, 105). The ultimate goal of these restructuring and renewal efforts must be to bring teachers, parents, and children, into a closer, intimate covenant related to their roles in promoting healthy human beings (9).

Unfortunately, in far too many cases in the past, energy has been spent on promoting isolationism (internalized as ethnocentric values) as opposed to partnership skills (70). Whatever structural changes are encouraged in families and schools, *teachers and parents need training on how to work with each other in partnerships endeavors.* This need must initially be addressed within both the preservice and in-service education of teachers. Integral in this training are several features that should promote a school-family and parent-teacher partnership approach to teaching and learning: teaching philosophy, parent/family life skills, parent-involvement skills, communication skills, teaming skills, and school-family-community linkage skills (114). Ultimately, this process should be extended to include teachers and parents in joint learning experiences that focus on issues and skills for developing partnerships. This process should promote a better understanding of the roles and relationships that need to be supported and integrated into parent-child-teacher interactions. Further, it should lead to the integration of teaming as a way of promoting children's success within the family and school (57, 59).

A crucial part of this partnership training should relate to the roles parents and teachers actually perform as well as to the interface roles they need to support in each other in order to have successful partnerships. This calls for teachers to acquire better insights into what parents do and confront on a daily basis, and for parents to interact more with teachers in classrooms in order to gain perspectives about the complexities they face in trying to create quality environments for young children (40, 105). This parent-teacher interactive participation in each other's roles does indeed promote partnership attitudes that help create a context for positive relationships (114). Yet to achieve this process it is necessary to restructure the personnel and emphases within the classroom ecology, perhaps developing a highly trained parapro-fessional who serves as a home-school leader to assure that these role exchanges do indeed take place.

Finally, public domain work and family policies need to be reorganized so as to support and promote teacher-parent partnerships. Providing parents with paid leave time to attend conferences to participate in classroom learning activities with their children, and to engage in planning work with teachers is one example of a desired practice (40). Providing teachers with time to plan and work with parents is another example of policy directions needed to support partnership efforts (114). Additional policies and practices that need attention include citizen involvement in activities that support parent involvement, school board policymaking that includes parent-teacher input on school reforms, and industry involvement in developing workplace practices that encourage parent involvement in the schools (115). Ultimately, successful teacher-parent partnerships in early childhood education are intimately linked to a responsive public policy environment.

BIBLIOGRAPHY

1. Anastasiow, N. "Should Parenting Education Be Mandatory?" *Topics in Early Childhood Special Education* 8, no. 1 (1988): 60–72.
2. Ascher, C. "Improving the School-Home Connection for Poor and Minority Urban Students." *Urban Review* 20 (1988): 115–21.
3. Atkinson, H. "A Report on the Needs of Homeless Parents and Children to the Advisory Council of Rainbow House." Columbia, S.C., November 1990.
4. Ball, R. "Ideas: Parent-School Involvement." *Dimensions* 14, no. 1 (1985): 15–18.
5. Bauch, J. "Parent Involvement Using High Tech for Maximum Impact." Research paper presented at the annual conference of the Southern Association on Children Under Six. Birmingham, Ala., 1988; 6 pp.
6. Becker, H., and Epstein, J. "Parent Involvement: A Study of Teacher Practices." *Elementary School Journal* 83 (1982): 85–102.
7. Bettelheim, B. *A Good Enough Parent.* New York: Alfred A. Knopf, 1987.
8. Bjorklund, G., and Burger, C. "Making Conferences Work for Parents, Teachers, and Young Children." *Young Children* 42, no. 2 (1987): 26–33.
9. Blazer, D. *Faith Development in Early Childhood.* Kansas City, Mo.: Sheed and Ward, 1989.
10. Bloom, B. *Developing Talent in Young People.* New York: Ballantine Books, 1985.
11. Boss, P. *Family Stress Management.* Newbury Park, Calif.: Sage, 1988.
12. Burchard, J., and Burchard, S. *Prevention of Delinquent Behavior.* Newbury Park, Calif.: Sage, 1987.
13. Burkett, C. "Effects of Frequency of Home Visits on Achievement of Preschool Students in a Home-Based Early Childhood Education Program." *Journal of Educational Research* 76, no. 1 (1982): 41–44.

14. Burland. J. "Dysfunctional Parenthood in a Deprived Population." In *Parenthood: A Psychodynamic Perspective,* edited by R. Cohen, B. Cohler, and S. Weissman, New York: Guilford Press, 1984.
15. Cataldo, C. *Parent Education for Early Childhood.* New York: Teachers College Press, 1987.
16. Chauvkin, N. "Debunking the Myth About Minority Parents." *Educational Horizons* 67, no. 4 (1989): 119–23.
17. Clay, J. "Working with Lesbian and Gay Parents and Their Children." *Young Children* 45, no. 3 (1990): 31–35.
18. Cochran, M., and Henderson, C. *Family Matters: Evaluation of the Parental Empowerment Program.* Ithaca, N.Y.: Cornell University (Final Report to the National Institute of Education), 1985.
19. Coleman, J. "Families and Schools." *Educational Researcher* 16 (1987): 32–38.
20. Comer, J. "Parental Participation in the Schools." *Phi Delta Kappan* 67 (1986): 442–46.
21. Darling, S. *Family Literacy Project.* Louisville, Ky.: The Kenan Trust Family Literacy Project, 1989.
22. Davies, D. "Schools Reaching Out: Family, School, and Community Partnerships for Student Success." *Phi Delta Kappan* 72 (1991): 383–88.
23. Dunst, C., and Trivette, C. "A Family Systems Model of Early Intervention with Handicapped and Developmentally At-Risk Children." In *Parent Education as Early Childhood Intervention,* edited by D. Powell. Norwood, N.J.: Ablex, 1988.
24. Duval, E. *Marriage and Family Development.* Philadelphia, Pa: Lippincott, 1977.
25. DeWolf, M. "Cable Show Gives Classwork a Boost." *USA Today,* 17 October 1990, p. 7-A.
26. Eddowes, A., and Hranitz, J. "Educating Children of the Homeless." *Childhood Education* 65, no. 4 (1989): 197–200.
27. Edelman, M. *Families in Peril: An Agenda for Social Change.* Cambridge: Harvard University Press, 1987.
28. Engstrom, L. "The Minnesota Experience with Family-Centered Early Childhood Programs." *Community Education Journal* (January 1988): 312–14.

29. Epstein, J. *Single Parents and the Schools: The Effect of Marital Status on Parent and Teacher Evaluations.* Baltimore, Md,: Center for Social Organization of Schools, The John Hopkins University, 1984.

30. ___."School Policy and Parent Involvement: Research Results." *Educational Horizons* 62 (1984): 70–72.

31. ___."Home and School Connections in Schools of the Future: Implications of Research On Parent Involvement." *Peabody Journal of Education* 62 (1985): 18–41.

32. ___."Paths to Partnership: What Can We Learn from Federal, State, District, and School Initiatives?" *Phi Delta Kappan* 72 (1991): 344–49.

33. Etlin, M. "Schools Reach Out to Parents." *NEA Today,* September 1990.

34. Fantini, M. *Parenting in a Multicultural Society.* New York: Longman, 1982.

35. Fraiberg, L. *Selected Writings of Selma Fraiberg.* Columbus, Ohio: Ohio State University Press, 1987.

36. Freedman, S. *Focus on Parents: Strategies for Increasing the Involvement of Underrepresented Families in Education.* Quincy, Mass.: Massachusetts Department of Education, 1989.

37. Galinsky, E. *The Six Stages of Parenthood.* Reading, Mass.: Addison-Wesley, 1987.

38. ___. "Parents and Teachers/Caregivers: Sources of Tension, Sources of Support." *Young Children* 43, no. 3 (1988): 4 12.

39. ___. "Why Are Some Teacher-Parent Relationships Clouded with Difficulties?" *Young Children* 45, no. 5 (1990): 2–3, 38–39.

40. ___. "Raising Children in the 1990's: The Challenges for Parents, Educators, and Business." *Young Children* 45, no. 2 (1990): 2–3, 67–69.

41. Garbarino, J. *Children and Families in the Social Environment.* New York: Aldine, 1982.

42. Garfinkle, I., and McLanahan, S. *Single Mothers and Their Children: A New American Dilemma.* Washington, D.C.: Urban Institute Press, 1986.

43. Gelles, R., and Straus, M. *Intimate Violence: The Causes and Consequences of Abuse in the American Family.* New York: Simon & Schuster, 1988.

44. Gordon, I. *Research Report of Parent Oriented Home-Based Early Childhood Education Programs*. Gainesville, Fla.: Institute for Human Development, University of Florida, 1977.

45. Gottfried, A. *Home Environment and Early Cognitive Development: Longitudinal Research*. New York: Academic Press, 1984.

46. Graves, S. "The Relationship of Parental Locus of Control, Interpersonal Support, and the Young Child's Level of Developmental Functioning in a Preschool Setting." Ph.D. diss., University of South Carolina, 1986.

47. Greenspan, S., and Greenspan, N. *First Feelings*. New York: Viking, 1985.

48. Hall, J. "Family Groups: A Link Between Parents and Preschool." *Dimensions* 17, no. 4 (1989): 4–7.

49. Halpern, R. "Major Social and Demographic Trends Affecting Young Families: Implications for Early Childhood Care and Education." *Young Children* 42, no. 6 (1987): 34–40.

50. Harisman, B. "Parents as Teachers—The Right Fit for Missouri." *Educational Horizons* 67 (1989): 35–39.

51. Haskins, R., and Adams, D. *Parent Education and Public Policy*. Norwood, N.J.: Ablex, 1983.

52. Heinecke, C., Beckwith, L., and Thompson, A. "Early Intervention in the Family System: A Framework." *Infant Mental Health Journal* 9 (1988): 11–141.

53. Henderson, A. *Parent Participation: The Evidence Grows*. Columbia, Md.: National Committee for Citizens in Education, 1981.

54. ___. "Parents Are a School's Best Friend." *Phi Delta Kappan* 70, no. 2 (1988): 148–53.

55. Herrera, J., and Wooden, S. "Some Thoughts About Effective Parent-School Communication." *Young Children* 43, no. 6 (1988): 78–80.

56. Holloway, M. *Building an Early Childhood Education Parent-Teacher Partnership*. Raleigh, N.C.: Raleigh Public Schools, 1988.

57. Hopman, W. "An Interactional Approach to Parent Training." *Childhood Education* 65 (1989): 167–71.

58. Irvine, D. *Parent Involvement Affects Children's Cognitive Growth*. Albany, N.Y.: Division of Research, Department of Education, 1979. Monograph.

59. Ispa, J., Gray, M., and Thornburg, K. "Parents, Teachers and Day Care Children: Patterns of Interconnection." *Journal of Research in Childhood Education* 3, no. 1 (1988): 76–84.

60. Jaffe, S., and Viertel, J. *Becoming Parents: Preparing for the Emotional Changes of First-Time Parenthood.* New York: Atheneum, 1980.

61. Johnson, J., and Martin, C. "Parents' Beliefs and Home Learning Environments." In *Parental Belief Systems: The Psychological Consequences on Children,* edited by I. Sigel. Hillsdale, N.J.: Lawrence Erlbaum Associates, 1985.

62. Kagan, S. "Home-School Linkages: History's Legacy and the Family Support Movement." In *America's Family Support Program's Perspectives and Prospects,* edited by S. Kagan; D. Powell; B. Weissbourd; and E. Zigler. New Haven, Conn.: Yale University Press, 1987.

63. Kerr, M., and Bowen, M. *Family Evaluation.* New York: W.W. Norton, 1988.

64. Klaus, M., and Robertson, M. *Birth, Interaction, and Attachment.* Skillman, N.J.: Johnson & Johnson, 1982.

65. Knowler, K. "Orienting Parents and Volunteers to the Classroom." *Young Children* 44, no. 1 (1988): 9–15.

66. Kotre, J., and Hall, E. *Seasons of Life: Our Dramatic Journey from Birth to Death.* Boston: Little, Brown & Co., 1990.

67. Lancaster, J. "The Evolution of the Human Family." In *The Lives of Families,* edited by K. Powers. Atlanta, Ga: Humanics Press, 1985.

68. LaRossa, R. *Becoming a Parent.* Newbury, Calif.: Sage, 1986.

69. Levenstein, P. *Messages from the Home: The Mother-Child Home Program and the Prevention of School Disadvantage.* Columbus: Ohio State University Press, 1988.

70. Lightfoot, S. *Worlds Apart: Relationships Between Families and School.* New York: Basic Books, 1978.

71. Lueder, D., and Bertrand, J. "Implementing Family/School Partnerships in Distressed Communities: A Critical Analysis of Successful Programs." Paper presented at the AERA Annual Conference. San Francisco, Calif.: American Educatonal Research Association, 1989.

72. Magid, K., and McKelvey, C. *High Risk: Children Without a Conscience.* New York: Bantam, 1988.

73. Manning, L. "Involving Fathers During the Early Years." *Dimensions* 17, no. 1 (1988): 13–14.

74. Marklein, M. "Help with Homework—On the House." *USA Today,* 17 October 1990: 7–A.

75. Mavrogenes, N. "Helping Parents Help Their Children Become Literate." *Young Children* 45, no. 4 (1990): 4–9.

76. Merina, A. "Parents Become Partners Right from the Start." *NEA Today* September 1990: 29.

77. Milardo, R. *Families and Social Networks.* Newbury Park, Calif.: Sage, 1988.

78. Minner, S. "Alternative Methods of Communicating with Parents." *Academic Therapy* 24, no. 5 (1989): 619–24.

79. Morgan, E. "Talking with Parents When Concerns Come Up." *Young Children* 44, no. 2 (1989): 52–56.

80. Morrison, G. *Parent Involvement in the Home, School, and Community.* Columbus, Ohio: Merrill, 1978.

81. Mueller, V. "Choice: The Parents' Perspective." *Phi Delta Kappan* 68, no. 10 (1987): 761.

82. Nichols, M. "The Nurturing Center." Columbia, S.C., 1990. Mimeo.

83. O'Brien, S. "Teachers and Parents Now Play on the Same Team." *Childhood Education* 66, no. 2 (1989): 106–7.

84. Olds, D.; Henderson, C.; Chamberlin, R.; and Tatlebaum, R. "Improving the Delivery of Prenatal Care and Outcomes of Pregnancy: A Randomized Trial of Nurse Home Visitation." *Pediatrics* 77 (1986): 16–28.

85. Parke, R. *Fathers.* Cambridge: Harvard University Press, 1981.

86. Pence, A. *Ecological Research with Children and Families.* New York: Teachers College Press, 1988.

87. Pizzo, P. "Family-Centered Head Start for Infants and Toddlers: A Renewed Direction for Project Head Start." *Young Children* 45, no. 6 (1990): 30–36.

88. Pooley, L., and Littel, J. *Family Resource Program Builder.* Chicago, Ill.: Family Resource Coalition, 1986.

89. Popenoe, D. *Disturbing the Nest: Family Change and Decline in Modern Societies.* New York: Aldine de Gruyter, 1988.

90. Potter, G. "Parent Participation in the Language Arts." *Language Arts* 66 (1989): 21–22.

91. Powell, D. *Parent Education as Early Childhood Intervention.* Norwood, N.J.: Ablex, 1988.

92. ___. *Families and Early Childhood Programs.* Washington, D.C.: National Association for the Education of Young Children, 1989.

93. ___. "Home Visiting in the Early Years: Policy and Program Design Decisions." *Young Children* 45, no. 6 (1990): 65–73.

94. Power, T. "Perceptions of Competence: How Parents and Teachers View Each Other." *Psychology in the Schools* 22 (1985): 68–78.

95. Rich, D. *The Forgotten Factor in School Success: The Family.* Washington, D.C.: Home and School Institute, 1985.

96. ___. *Schools and Families: Issues and Actions.* Washington, D.C.: National Education Association, 1987.

97. ___. *Teachers and Parents: An Adult-to-Adult Approach.* Washington, D.C.: National Education Association, 1987.

98. ___. *MegaSkills: How Families Can Help Children Succeed.* Boston: Houghton Mifflin, 1988.

99. Robinson, B. "The Teacher's Role in Working with Children of Alcoholic Parents." *Young Children* 45, no.4 (1990): 68–73.

100. Rohner, R. *The Warmth Dimension: Foundations of Parental Acceptance-Rejection Theory.* Newbury Park, Calif.: Sage, 1986.

101. Rossi, A., and Rossi, P. *Of Human Bonding.* New York: Aldine de Gruyter, 1990.

102. Sagan, L. *The Health of Nations.* New York: Basic Books, 1987.

103. Sasserath, V., and Hoekelman, R. *Minimizing High-Risk Parenting.* Skillman, N.J.: Johnson & Johnson, 1983.

104. Schaefer, E. "Parent and Child Correlates of Parental Modernity." In *Parental Belief Systems: The Psychological Consequences for Children,* edited by I. Sigel. Hillsdale, N.J.: Lawrence Erlbaum Associates, 1985.

105. ___. "Parent-Professional Interaction: Research, Parental, Professional, and Policy Perspectives." In *Parent Education and Public Policy,* edited by R. Haskins and D. Adams, Norwood, N.J.: Ablex, 1982.

106. Schoor, L., and Schoor, D. *Within Our Reach: Breaking the Cycle of Disadvantage.* New York: Doubleday, 1988.

107. Shields, P., and David, J. *The Implementation of Family Math in Five Community Agencies.* Berkeley, Calif.: EQUALS Program, Lawrence Hall of Science, 1988.

108. Sigel, I. *Parental Belief Systems: The Psychological Consequence for Children.* Hillsdale, N.J.: Lawrence Erlbaum Associates, 1985.

109. Sinclair, R. *A Two-Way Street: Home-School Cooperation in Educational Decisionmaking.* Boston: Institute for Responsive Education, 1980.

110. Stinnett, N. *Family Strengths: Roots of Well-Being.* Lincoln, Nebr.: University of Nebraska Press, 1981.

111. ___. *Family Strengths: Positive Support Systems.* Lincoln, Nebr.: University of Nebraska Press, 1982.

112. Suransky, V. *The Erosion of Childhood.* Chicago: University of Chicago Press, 1982.

113. Swick, K., and Duff, E. *The Parent-Teacher Bond.* Dubuque, Iowa: Kendall-Hunt, 1978.

114. Swick, K. *Inviting Parents into the Young Child's World.* Champaign, Ill.: Stipes, 1984.

115. ___. *Perspectives on Understanding and Working with Families.* Champaign, Ill.: Stipes, 1987.

116. ___. *Parents and Teachers as Discipline Shapers.* Washington, D.C.: National Education Association, 1987.

117. ___. "Teacher Reports on Parental Efficacy/Involvement Relationships." *Instructional Psychology* 14 (1987): 125–32.

118. ___. "Parental Efficacy/Involvement Relationships: Influences on Children." *Childhood Education* 64, no. 1 (1988): 62–67.

119. ___. "Parental Efficacy and Social Competence in Young Children." *Dimensions* 17, no. 3 (1989): 25–26.

120. ___. "Computer Education for Parents of Preschoolers." *Educational Technology* (May 1990): 39–45.

121. ___. *First: A Rural Teacher-Parent Partnership for School Success.* Final report to the U.S. Office of Education (First Division), Columbia, South Carolina, 1991.

122. Swick, K., and McKnight, S. "Characteristics of Kindergarten Teachers Who Promote Parent Involvement." *Early Childhood Research Quarterly* 4, no. 1 (1989): 19–30.

123. Taylor, D. *Family Literacy.* London: Heinemann, 1982.

124. Tivnan, T. "Lessons from the Evaluation of the Brookline Early Education Project." In *Evaluating Family Programs,* edited by H. Weiss and F. Jacobs. New York: Aldine de Gruyter, 1988.

125. Vartuli, S., and Rogers, P. "Parent-Child Learning Centers." *Dimensions* 14, no. 1 (1985): 8–10.

126. Walberg, H.; Bakalis, M.; Bast, J.; and Baer, S. "Reconstructing the Nation's Worst Schools." *Phi Delta Kappan* 70, no. 10 (1989): 802–5.

127. Wallerstein, J., and Blakeslee, S. *Second Chances: Men, Women, and Children a Decade After Divorce.* New York: Tickner & Fields, 1989.
128. Weiss, F., and Jacobs, S. *Evaluating Family Programs.* New York: Aldine de Gruyter, 1988.
129. White, B. *Educating the Infant and Toddler.* Lexington, Mass.: D.C. Heath, 1988.
130. Wilson, J., and Herrnstein, R. *Crime and Human Nature.* New York: Simon & Schuster, 1985.

ATE DUE